CHILTON'S *New*
Repair and Tune-Up Guide

FOR THE

YAMAHA

PREPARED BY THE AUTOMOTIVE DEPARTMENT OF
CHILTON BOOK COMPANY

JOHN D. KELLY, *Managing Editor*
PETER J. MEYER, *Ass't Managing Editor*
SVANTE E. MOSSBERG, *Senior Editor, Motorcycles*
JAMES H. JOHNSON, *Editor*
MICHAEL S. YAMPOLSKY, *Editor*

Illustrated

CHILTON BOOK COMPANY
Radnor, Pennsylvania

MEMBER
MIC
MOTORCYCLE INDUSTRY COUNCIL

ACKNOWLEDGMENTS

Yamaha International Corp.
Buena Park, California 90620
Bellmawr, New Jersey 08030

Japan Motor Industrial Federation
Tokyo, Japan

Contents

Chapter 1 Model Identification and Description **1**

Development and History, 1
Major Improvements and Model
   Changes, 12

General Specifications, 13

Chapter 2 Maintenance **22**

Oil Changes and Lubrication, 22
Cleaning, 24
Two-Stroke Decarbonization, 25
Service Checks and Adjustments, 26

Brakes, 28
Storage, 31
Maintenance Data, 33

Chapter 3 Tune-Up **34**

Two-Stroke Tuning, 34
Ignition Point and Timing, 34
Spark Plugs, 37
Twin Carburetor Synchronization, 38
Throttle Cable Adjustment, 38
Oil Pump Cable Adjustment, 39
Minimum Oil Pump Stroke, 40
XS1/XS2 Tuning, 40
Cam Chain Tensioner, 40
Ignition Points and Timing, 41

Spark Plugs, 42
Valve Clearance, 42
Carburetor Idle Speed and Mixture, 43
Carburetor Synchronization, 43
Throttle Cable Adjustment, 43
Tune-Up Analysis, 43
Millimeters to Inches, 45
Spark Plug Comparison Chart, 46
Tune-Up Specifications, 51

Chapter 4 Engine and Transmission **54**

Two-Stroke Models, 54
Transmission Description, 56
Engine Removal, 56
Engine Installation, 63
Engine Disassembly and Repair, 64
Cylinder Head, 64
Cylinder, 64
Piston, 66
Right Crankcase Cover, 68
Clutch, 69
Primary Drive Gear, 71

Kickstarter Mechanism, 72
Rotary Valve, 72
Countershaft Sprocket, 73
Crankcase, Shifter and Transmission, 73
Piston Skirt Clearance Specifications, 92
XS1/XS2 Piston Ring Specifications, 93
XS1/XS2 Cam Lobe Specifications, 93
XS1/XS2 Valve Seat Specifications, 93
XS1/XS2 Valve Guide Specifications, 93
XS1/XS2 Valve Spring Specifications, 93
Torque Specifications, 94

Chapter 5 Lubrication Systems **95**

Two-Stroke Models, 95

Autolube Pump Output, 98

Chapter 6 Fuel Systems **100**

Two-Stroke Models, 100
XS1/XS2, 106

XS1/XS2 Carburetor Specifications, 108
Two-Stroke Carburetor
   Specifications, 109

Chapter 7 Electrical Systems **110**

Magneto, 110
DC Generator, 110
Starter Generator, 111
Alternator, 111

Component Tests, 113
Electrical Wiring Color Codes, 117
Electrical Specifications, 117

Chapter 8 Chassis **124**

Front Wheel, 124

Rear Wheel, 126
Front Fork (Enduro Type), 127

Front Fork (Standard Telescopic
   Type), 128
Rear Shock Absorbers, 129
Rear Swing Arm, 129

Chapter 9   Performance and Racing Modifications **130**

     Improving Standard Performance, 130   Factory Roadracing Models, 142
     Racing Modifications, 133   Factory Motocross Models, 144

Chapter 10   Troubleshooting **146**

     Two-Stroke Performance   Four-Stroke Performance
       Troubleshooting, 146   Troubleshooting, 150
     Autolube Troubleshooting, 149

1 ● Model Identification Description

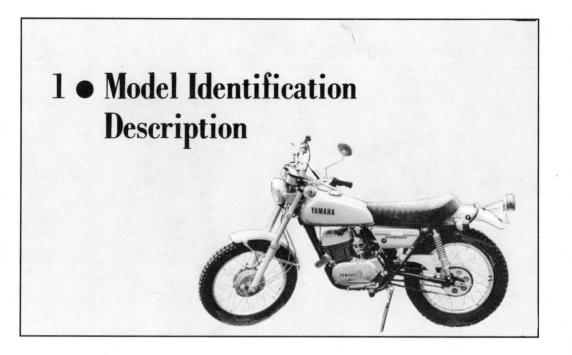

Development History

Yamaha Motor Company, Ltd. was established in 1955 as a small subsidiary of Nippon Gakki, Ltd., the world's largest piano manufacturer. The firm's entrance into the field of motorcycle production was hardly considered a serious threat by the giants of the industry, but after the first model was introduced and marketed later that same year, they quickly realized that Yamaha would soon be a formidable competitor.

The first Yamaha motorcycle was designated YA-1 and dubbed the "Red Dragonfly." It was styled after the famous BMW and was powered by a 125cc single-cylinder two-stroke engine. This first effort was such a success in Japan that, by 1959, the company was offering sports and utility models in 125, 175, and 250cc displacements. In 1960, their phenomenal growth continued, multiplying their original investment nearly thirty times and expanding their product line to include mopeds, boats, and outboard motors.

By that time, the Asian export market had already proven very profitable, but it wasn't until the early-to-mid-1960s that foreign sales really began to soar: America discovered the Japanese motorcycle and suddenly the demand for them became overwhelming.

The motorcycle industry's heated competition for this new market was eventually carried to the European Grand Prix circuit, where Yamaha and their rivals locked horns in a furious racing and development battle. Factory engineers worked frantically to provide faster and more powerful machines for the Grand Prix effort and, as a result, two-stroke motorcycle technology advanced by leaps and bounds and the Yamaha racing team won five world championships.

After development and thorough testing, the products of this racing program were employed on production machines: mainly, the rotary-valve in 1961, Autolube oil injection in 1963, and the five-port cylinder in 1968.

Meanwhile, Yamaha Motor Company, Ltd. continued to grow—building nine new plants in Japan, Taiwan, Mexico, Costa Rica, Ecuador, and Guatemala. In addition to achievement awards in motorcycle engineering, the company also received great acclaim for their design of the Toyota 2000 GT in 1966, and the introduction of Yamaha snowmobiles in 1968.

Most recently, the firm has built a new test facility in Japan and introduced a complete line of off-road Enduro and Motocross motorcycles. They have also expanded their street motorcycle offering by applying their Toyota 2000 GT experience to the construction of Yamaha's first four-stroke model—the XS1.

The Yamaha trademark of three crossed tuning forks has now become a familiar sight all over the world and serves as a subtle reminder of the firm's musical origin. Their motorcycle products currently range from the 58cc Mini-Enduro to racing's "dynamic duo," the 250cc

YJ2 Campus 60

YGS1T Trail 80

U5 Newport 50

YGS1 Sport 80

YL2 Rotary Jet 100

YA6 Santa Barbara 125

YL1 Twin Jet 100

YL2C Trailmaster 100

YDS3 Catalina 250

YM2C Scrambler 305

YCS1 Street 180

YM2 Cross Country 305

YDS5 Sport 250

YAS1C Twin Street Scrambler 125

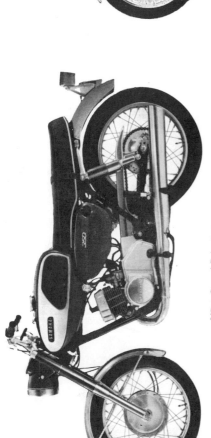

YR1 Grand Prix 350

YCS1C Twin Street Scrambler 180

YR2 Grand Prix 350

CT1 Enduro 175

DT1 Enduro 250

AT1 Enduro 125

R3 Grand Prix 350

HT1 Enduro 90

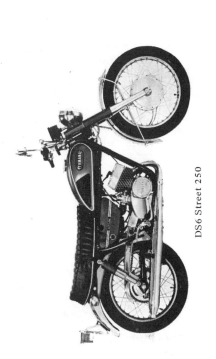

DS6 Street 250

HS 1 Twin Street 90

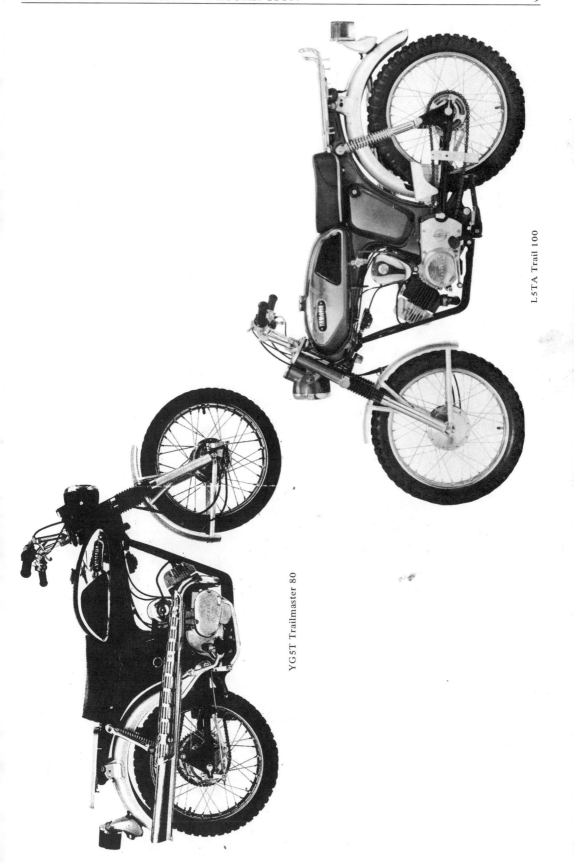

L5TA Trail 100

YG5T Trailmaster 80

CS3C Street Scrambler 200

RT1 Enduro 360

XS1 Street 650

R5 Street 350

TD and 350cc TR roadracers. There is a model to suit every enthusiast and each one reflects, as Yamahas always have, the ever-growing interests of the motorcycling public.

Major Improvements and Model Changes

1964, '65, '66

Introduction of the YL1 (98cc twin), YM1 (305cc twin) and Autolube oil injection on all models. With the new lubrication system and other improvements, the YJ1 (55cc rotary-valve single) became the YJ2 (58cc rotary-valve single), the YG1K (73cc rotary-valve single) became the YG1K (same) and YGS1/T, the YDS2 (246cc twin) became the YDS3/C and, with the addition of electric starting, the U5 (50cc rotary-valve single) and YA5 (123cc rotary-valve single) evolved into the U5E and YA6.

1967

Introduction of the YL2/C (97cc rotary-valve single), YCS1 (180cc twin), YR1 (348cc twin) and primary kickstarting on some models. With the addition of electric starting, the YL1 became the YL1E and the YDS3/C became the DS5. The new YL2/C and YCS1 were also equipped with electric starters.

1968

Introduction of the YAS1/C (124cc twin), DT1 Enduro (246cc single), and a new five-port cylinder design. The new cylinder was used on the DT1, YAS1/C, and the YR2/C (evolved from YR1). With the addition of electric starting and other changes, the YG1K and YGS1/T became the YG5T and the YCS1 became YCS1C.

1969

Introduction of the AT1 Enduro (123cc single with electric starting), CT1 Enduro (171cc single), and L5T (97cc rotary-valve single with electric starting and a two-range, three-speed transmission). The YAS1/C became the AS2C and the YG5T became the G5S (without elec-

tric starting). The DS5 of 1967 evolved into the DS6/C (without electric starting), the YR2/C into the newly styled R3 and the DT1 into the DT1B. The five-port cylinder was now used on all but the rotary-valve models.

1970

Introduction of the HS1 (89cc twin), HT1 Enduro (89cc single), RT1 Enduro (351cc single), XS1 (653cc SOHC four-stroke twin), and Keystone-type piston rings. The YCS1/C and R3 were completely revamped to produce the CS3C (195cc twin) and R5 (347cc twin). With new styling and internal improvements, the G5S, AT1, L5T, CT1, DT1B, and DS6/C became the G6S, AT1B, L5TA, CT1B, DT1C, and DS6B. The five-port cylinder was also used on the new HS1, HT1, and RT1.

1971

Introduction of the JT1 Mini-Enduro (58cc rotary-valve single). All 1971 models carried a last letter designation change from their 1970 versions. For example, the HT1 of 1970 became the HT1B in 1971, even though very few changes were made. The most significant improvements of the year were in the DT1E and RT1B: they were both equipped with identical frames and redesigned gearboxes, and the RT1B was fitted with a compression release.

1972

Introduction of reed valve induction on the AT2, CT2, DT2, RT2, and the new LT2 (100cc Enduro) and U7E (70cc Moped). The HS1 was enlarged to 97cc, restyled and designated LS2. The DS6 was completely revamped and designated DS7, and the JT1 Mini Enduro was made available in either street trim (JT2L) or purely off-road trim (JT2M). The XS1 was fitted with a front disc brake and electric starting, and was redesignated XS2.

Yamaha's racing stable has also been vastly improved and enlarged since the first production machines were introduced. The recent Motocross dirt bikes, as well as the Ascot scrambler and TD/TR roadracers, are covered in Performance and Racing Modification.

General Specifications

	U5/U5L	U5E	U7E	MJ2/MJ2T	YJ1	Early YJ2	Late YJ2
DIMENSIONS							
Net Weight	190	190	170	190	190	190	190
Overall Length (in)	77.7	71.1	—	67.5	72.4	71.3	71.3
Overall Width (in)	24.8	24.8	—	25.2	25.4	25.4	25.4
Overall Height (in)	37.2	37.2	—	37.5	38.4	38.4	88.4
Ground Clearance (in)	5.1	5.1	—	4.9	5.5	5.5	5.5
Wheelbase (in)	44.9	44.9	—	44.9	45.8	45.1	45.1
Tire Size (in): front	2.25 x 17	2.25 x 17	2.25 x 17	2.25 x 16	2.25 x 17	2.25 x 17	2.25 x 17
rear	2.25 x 17	2.25 x 17	2.50 x 17	2.25 x 16	2.25 x 17	2.25 x 17	2.25 x 17
ENGINE							
Displacement (cc)	50	50	72	55	55	58	58
No. of Cylinders	1	1	1	1	1	1	1
Bore X Stroke (mm)	40 x 40	40 x 40	47 x 42	42 x 40	42 x 40	42 x 42	42 x 42
Compression Ratio (:1)	6.8	6.8	6.8	7.4	7.1	6.6	7.5
Horsepower @ RPM	4.5 @ 6500	4.5 @ 6500	4.9 @ 6500	4.7 @ 6500	4.7 @ 6500	4.7 @ 6500	5.0 @ 7000
Torque @ RPM (ft lbs)	3.76 @ 5000	3.76 @ 5000	4.7 @ 4500	3.9 @ 6000	3.9 @ 6000	3.9 @ 6000	3.98 @ 6000
Fuel Induct. (RV, PP) ①	RV	RV	★	RV	RV	RV	RV
Carburetion (Mikuni)	VM14	VM14	VM15SC	VM14SC	VM14SC	VM14SC	VM16
Lubrication (PM, OI) ②	OI	OI	OI	PM	PM	OI	OI
TRANSMISSION							
Clutch	Auto	Auto	Auto	Auto/Manual	Manual	Manual	Manual
Reduction (pri/sec)	3.895/2.715	3.895/2.715	3.578/2.571	3.895/2.715	3.895/2.786	3.895/2.600	3.895/2.533
Transmission Ratio: 1st	3.083	3.083	3.250	3.083	3.083	3.083	3.083
2nd	1.722	1.722	1.833	1.824	1.882	1.882	1.882
3rd	1.174	1.174	1.200	1.227	1.333	1.338	1.333
4th	—	—	—	—	1.000	1.000	1.000
5th	—	—	—	—	—	—	—
ELECTRICS							
Ignition	Magneto	Generator	Generator	Generator	Magneto	Magneto	Magneto
Starting	Kick	Electric	Electric	Kick	Kick	Kick	Kick
PERFORMANCE							
Climbing Ability (deg)	20	20	—	14	15	18	18
Turning Radius (in)	69.0	69.0	—	68.9	71.2	71.2	71.2
Braking Dist. (ft @ mph)	9.8 @ 15	9.8 @ 18	—	22.8 @ 22	9.8 @ 15	9.8 @ 15	9.8 @ 15
Fuel Consump. (mpg @ mph)	200 @ 18	200 @ 18	—	220 @ 18	220 @ 18	220 @ 18	220 @ 18

① RV—rotary valve; PP—piston port.   *Reed valve.

② PM—premix; OI—oil injection.

General Specifications, continued

	JT1/JT2	MGIT	YGI/YGIK	YGIT/YGITK	YGSI/YGSIT	YG5T
DIMENSIONS						
Net Weight	121	190	190	190	190	175
Overall Length (in)	62.0	62.0	71.5	71.7	71.7	70.9
Overall Width (in)	27.6	29.7	24.6	29.8	24.6/30.5	31.7
Overall Height (in)	36.6	38.6	37.8	39.4	37.8/38.8	40.0
Ground Clearance (in)	6.3	5.5	5.9	5.9	5.9	6.3
Wheelbase (in)	45.1	45.1	45.1	45.1	45.1	46.3
Tire Size (in): front	2.50 x 15	2.50 x 16	2.50 x 17	2.50 x 17	2.50 x 17	2.50 x 17
rear	2.50 x 15	2.50 x 16	2.50 x 17	2.50 x 17	2.50 x 17	3.00 x 17
ENGINE						
Displacement (cc)	58	73	73	73	73	73
No. of Cylinders	1	1	1	1	1	1
Bore X Stroke (mm)	42 x 42	47 x 42	47 x 42	47 x 42	47 x 42	47 x 42
Compression Ratio (:1)	6.4	6.8	6.8	6.8	6.8	6.8
Horsepower @ RPM	4.5 @ 7500	7.7 @ 7500	7.7 @ 7500	7.7 @ 7500	8.0 @ 7500	6.6 @ 7000
Torque @ RPM (ft lbs)	3.62 @ 5500	5.06 @ 6500	5.06 @ 6500	5.06 @ 6500	5.78 @ 6500	5.2 @ 6000
Fuel Induct. (RV, PP)①	RV	RV	RV	RV	RV	RV
Carburetion (Mikuni)	Y16P(Teikei)	VM15SC-1	VM15SC-1	VM15SC-1	VM15SC-1	VM16SC
Lubrication (PM, OI)②	OI	PM	PM/OI	PM/OI	OI	OI
TRANSMISSION						
Clutch	Manual	Manual	Manual	Manual	Manual	Manual
Reduction (pri/sec)	3.895/3.154	3.895/2.467	3.895/2.467	3.895/2.467	3.895/2.467	3.895/2.740
Transmission Ratio: 1st	3.077	3.083	3.083	3.083	3.083	3.077
2nd	1.889	1.882	1.882	1.882	1.882	1.889
3rd	1.304	1.333	1.333	1.333	1.333	1.304
4th	1.038	1.000	1.000	1.000	1.000	0.963
5th	—	—	—	—	—	—
ELECTRICS						
Ignition	Magneto	Magneto	Magneto	Magneto	Magneto	Generator
Starting	Kick	Kick	Kick	Kick	Kick	Electric
PERFORMANCE						
Climbing Ability (deg)	22	20	20	20	20	30
Turning Radius (in)	59.1	59.9	70.1	71.2	70.1	70.9
Braking Dist. (ft @ mph)	24.6 @ 22	23 @ 22	23 @ 22	23 @ 22	23 @ 22	20 @ 22
Fuel Consump. (mpg @ mph)	176 @ 19	188 @ 19	188 @ 19	188 @ 19	131 @ 14	140 @ 25

① RV—rotary valve; PP—piston port.

② PM—premix; OI—oil injection.

General Specifications, continued

	G5S	G6S/G6SB/G7S	HTI/HTIB	HSI/HSIB	YL2	YL2C
DIMENSIONS						
Net Weight	170	170	190	199	200	200
Overall Length (in)	71.3	71.3	73.8	70.9	75.4	73.2
Overall Width (in)	31.1	31.1	35.4	30.3	28.1	28.1
Overall Height (in)	39.2	39.2	40.7	39.6	41.7	42.5
Ground Clearance (in)	5.3	5.3	8.9	6.1	5.5	7.9
Wheelbase (in)	45.9	45.9	48.0	47.0	46.9	48.5
Tire Size (in): front	2.50 x 17	2.50 x 17	2.75 x 18	2.50 x 18	2.50 x 18	3.00 x 18
rear	2.50 x 17	2.50 x 17	3.00 x 18	2.50 x 18	2.50 x 18	3.00 x 18
ENGINE						
Displacement (cc)	73	73	89	89	97	97
No. of Cylinders	1	1	1	2	1	1
Bore X Stroke (mm)	47 x 42	47 x 42	50 x 45.6	36.5 x 43	52 x 45.6	52 x 45.6
Compression Ratio (:1)	6.8	6.8	6.8	7.5	7.0	7.0
Horsepower @ RPM	4.9 @ 7500	4.9 @ 7500	8.5 @ 7500	4.9 @ 8000	9.5 @ 7500	9.5 @ 7500
Torque @ RPM (ft lbs)	4.1 @ 5500	4.1 @ 5500	6.5 @ 6500	3.1 @ 5500	6.8 @ 5500	7.24 @ 6000
Fuel Induct. (RV, PP)①	RV	RV	PP	PP	RV	RV
Carburetion (Mikuni)	VM16SC	VM16SC	VM20SC	VM16SC (2)	VM17SC	VM17SC
Lubrication (PM, OI)②	OI	OI	OI	OI	OI	OI
TRANSMISSION						
Clutch	Manual	Manual	Manual	Manual	Manual	Manual
Reduction (pri/sec)	3.895/2.643	3.895/2.643	3.895/3.590	3.895/3.077	3.895/2.335	3.895/2.335
Transmission Ratio: 1st	3.077	3.077	3.181	3.182	3.077	3.077
2nd	1.889	1.889	2.000	1.813	1.889	1.889
3rd	1.304	1.304	1.368	1.300	1.304	1.304
4th	0.963	0.963	1.000	1.045	0.963	0.963
5th	—	—	0.800	0.840	—	—
ELECTRICS						
Ignition	Magneto	Magneto	Magneto	Alternator	Generator	Generator
Starting	Kick	Kick	Kick	Kick	Kick	Electric
PERFORMANCE						
Climbing Ability (deg)	20	20	25	20	22	22
Turning Radius (in)	70.9	70.9	68.9	70.9	73.5	73.5
Braking Dist. (ft @ mph)	21 @ 22	23 @ 22	23 @ 22	21 @ 22	22.6 @ 21.8	22.6 @ 21.8
Fuel Consump. (mpg @ mph)	190 @ 25	190 @ 25	153 @ 25	153 @ 25	140 @ 25	140 @ 25

① RV—rotary valve; PP—piston port.

② PM—premix; OI—oil injection.

General Specifications, continued

	YL2CM 3	L5T/L5TA	LT2	LS2	YL1/NL1E	YA5	YA6	AT1/AT1B/AT1C
DIMENSIONS								
Net Weight	200	198	187	209	180	245	245	218
Overall Length (in)	732	70.9	—	—	71.6	74.2	75.6	77.2
Overall Width (in)	28.1	31.7	—	—	24.8	26.8	28.5	35.8
Overall Height (in)	42.5	40.2	—	—	37.3	37.6	41.1	42.9
Ground Clearance (in)	6.9	6.3	—	—	5.1	4.9	5.3	8.9
Wheelbase (in)	48.5	46.3	—	—	45.1	49.2	49.0	50.6
Tire Size (in): front	3.00 x 18	2.75 x 17	2.75 x 18	2.50 x 18	2.50 x 17	3.00 x 16	3.00 x 16	3.00 x 18
rear	3.00 x 18	3.00 x 17	3.00 x 18	2.50 x 18	2.50 x 17	3.00 x 16	3.00 x 16	3.25 x 18
ENGINE								
Displacement (cc)	97	97	97	97	98	123	123	123
No. of Cylinders	1	1	1	2	2	1	1	1
Bore X Stroke (mm)	52 x 45.6	52 x 45.6	52 x 45.6	38 x 40	38 x 43	56 x 50	56 x 50	56 x 50
Compression Ratio (:1)	6.6	6.8	6.9	7.0	7.1	6.75	6.8	7.1
Horsepower @ RPM	9.7 @ 7000	8.0 @ 6000	10 @ 7500	10.5 @ 8000	9.5 @ 8500	11 @ 6700	11 @ 6700	11.5 @ 7500
Torque @ RPM (ft lbs)	7.24 @ 6000	6.9 @ 5000	7.0 @ 7000	6.95 @ 7500	6.0 @ 8000	9 @ 5000	9 @ 5000	8.5 @ 7000
Fuel Induct. (RV, PP) ①	RV	RV	★	PP	PP	RV	RV	PP
Carburetion (Mikuni)	VM20SC	VM20SC	VM20SH	VM17SC	VM16SC (2)	M21SI	VM22SC	VM24SH
Lubrication (PM, OI) ②	OI	OI	OI	OI	OI	PM	OI	OI
TRANSMISSION								
Clutch	Manual	Manual	Manual	Manual	Manual	Manual	Manual	Manual
Reduction (pri/sec)	3.895/2.334	3.895/2.310	3.895/3.590	3.894/3.000	3.895/2.335	2.785/2.730	3.833/2.600	3.895/3.214
Transmission Ratio: 1st	3.077	2.833 (h) 4.647 (l)	3.181	3.181	3.077	2.965	2.533	3.182
2nd	1.889	1.647 (h) 2.702 (l)	2.000	1.812	1.889	1.794	1.524	2.000
3rd	1.304	1.000 (h) 1.640 (l)	1.386	1.300	1.304	1.291	1.120	1.368
4th	0.963	—	1.000	1.045	0.963	1.000	0.828	1.000
5th	—	—	0.800	0.840	—	—	—	0.800
ELECTRICS								
Ignition	Generator	Generator	Alternator	Alternator	Generator	Generator	Generator	Generator
Starting	Electric	Electric	Kick	Kick	Kick/Electric	Electric	Electric	Electric
PERFORMANCE								
Climbing Ability (deg)	22	35	—	—	20	33	20	30
Turning Radius (in)	73.5	70.9	—	—	70.1	74.8	72.0	75.1
Braking Dist. (ft @ mph)	22.6 @ 21.8	27.9 @ 22	—	—	23 @ 22	40 @ 32	23 @ 22	58.3 @ 31
Fuel Con. (mpg @ mph)	140 @ 25	165 @ 19	—	—	153 @ 19	180 @ 20.4	183 @ 19	141 @ 25

① RV—rotary valve; PP—piston port. ★ Reed valve. ⑩ AT1—Piston port; AT2—Reed valve.

② PM—premix; OI—oil injection. ⑧ AT1—11.5 @ 7500; AT2—13 @ 7000. ⑪ AT1—3.214; AT2—3.000.

③ YL2C after ser #550101. ⑨ AT1—8.5 @ 7000; AT2—10 @ 6000.

General Specifications, continued

	YAS1/YASIC AS2C	CT1/CTIB/ CTIC/CT2	YCSIC	YCSI	CS3C	CS3B/CS5
DIMENSIONS						
Net Weight	220	211	260	260	262	258
Overall Length (in)	73.0	77.4	75.6	75.6	76.0	76.0
Overall Width (in)	31.9	35.8	30.1	30.1	32.1	32.1
Overall Height (in)	39.6	43.1	39.2	39.2	40.2	40.2
Ground Clearance (in)	5.9	9.1	6.1	6.1	6.9	6.9
Wheelbase (in)	47.2	50.6	49.0	49.0	49.0	49.0
Tire Size (in): front	2.75 x 18	3.25 x 18	2.75 x 18	3.00 x 18	2.75 x 18	2.75 x 18
rear	3.00 x 18	3.50 x 18	3.00 x 18	3.00 x 18	3.00 x 18	3.00 x 18
ENGINE						
Displacement (cc)	124	171	180	180	195	195
No. of Cylinders	2	1	2	2	2	2
Bore X Stroke (mm)	43 x 43	66 x 50	50 x 46	50 x 46	52 x 46	52 x 46
Compression Ratio (:1)	7.0	6.8	7.0	6.8	6.2	7.1
Horsepower @ RPM	15.2 @ 8500	⑫	21 @ 7500	21 @ 8000	22 @ 7500	22 @ 7500
Torque @ RPM (ft lbs)	9.4 @ 7500	⑬	14.6 @ 7000	14.6 @ 7000	15.7 @ 7000	15.7 @ 7000
Fuel Induction (RV, PP)①	PP	⑭	PP	PP	PP	PP
Carburetion (Mikuni)	VM17SC(2)	VM24SH	VM20SC (2)	VM18SC (2)	VM20SC(2)	VM20SC (2)
Lubrication (PM, OI)②	OI	OI	OI	OI	OI	OI
TRANSMISSION						
Clutch	Manual	Manual	Manual	Manual	Manual	Manual
Reduction (pri/sec)	3.895/2.600	3.895/2.812	3.313/2.667	3.313/2.466	3.313/2.857	3.313/2.857
Transmission Ratio: 1st	3.182	3.182	2.833	2.833	2.833	2.833
2nd	1.875	2.000	1.875	1.875	1.875	1.875
3rd	1.300	1.368	1.421	1.421	1.421	1.421
4th	1.045	1.000	1.045	1.045	1.045	1.045
5th	0.840	0.800	0.840	0.840	0.840	0.840
ELECTRICS						
Ignition	Alternator	Magneto	Generator	Generator	Generator	Generator
Starting	Kick	Kick	Electric	Electric	Electric	Electric
PERFORMANCE						
Climbing Ability (deg)	23.5	32	23	23	25	25
Turning Radius (in)	69.0	74.8	80.8	80.8	80.7	80.7
Braking Dist. (ft @ mph)	38 @ 30	58.3 @ 31	39 @ 31	39 @ 31	36 @ 31	36 @ 31
Fuel Consump. (mpg @ mph)	150 @ 25	129 @ 25	130 @ 25	130 @ 25	118 @ 25	118 @ 25

① RV—rotary valve; PP—piston port.

② PM—premix; OI—oil injection.

⑫ CT1—15.6 @ 7000; CT2—16 @ 7500

⑬ CT1—11.9 @ 6500; CT2—11.9 @ 6000

⑭ CT1—Piston port; CT2—Reed valve

General Specifications, continued

	DTI	DTIB/DTIS	DTIC	DTIE/DT2	YD3	YDTI ④
DIMENSIONS						
Net Weight (lbs.)	232	232	232	⑮	337	345
Overall Length (in)	78.3	81.1	81.1	78.3	73.0	78.3
Overall Width (in)	28.9	28.9	28.9	28.9	28.7	28.9
Overall Height (in)	42.5	42.5	42.5	43.5	38.2	42.5
Ground Clearance (in)	9.6	9.6	9.6	10.0	5.3	5.1
Wheelbase (in)	50.8	53.6	53.6	54.7	49.4	50.8
Tire Size (in): front	3.25 x 19	3.25 x 19	3.25 x 19	3.25 x 19	3.25 x 16	2.75 x 18
rear	400 x 18	400 x 18	4.00 x 18	4.00 x 18	3.25 x 16	3.00 x 18
ENGINE						
Displacement (cc)	246	246	246	246	247	247
No. of Cylinders	1	1	1	1	2	2
Bore X Stroke (mm)	70 x 64	70 x 64	70 x 64	70 x 64	54 x 54	54 x 54
Compression Ratio (:1)	6.8	6.8	6.4	6.4	7.0	7.0
Horsepower @ RPM	21 @ 6000	21 @ 6000	23 @ 7000	⑯	17 @ 6000	17 @ 6000
Torque @ RPM (ft lbs)	16.8 @ 5000	16.8 @ 5000	17.5 @ 6500	⑰	17.8 @ 4500	17.8 @ 4500
Fuel Induct. (RV, PP) ①	PP	PP	PP	⑱	PP	PP
Carburetion (Mikuni)	VM26SH	VM26SH	VM26SH	VM26SH	VM20SC (2)	VM20SC (2)
Lubrication (PM, OI) ②	OI	OI	OI	OI	PM	PM
TRANSMISSION						
Clutch	Manual	Manual	Manual	Manual	Manual	Manual
Reduction (pri/sec)	3.095/2.933	3.095/2.933	3.095/3.143	3.095/3.143	3.250/2.060	3.250/2.060
Transmission Ratio: 1st	2.231	2.231	2.533	2.533	2.500	2.500
2nd	1.624	1.624	1.789	1.789	1.530	1.530
3rd	1.211	1.211	1.304	1.304	1.227	1.227
4th	1.000	1.000	1.000	1.000	0.960	0.960
5th	0.826	0.826	0.767	0.767	—	—
ELECTRICS						
Ignition	Magneto	Magneto	Magneto	Magneto	Generator	Generator
Starting	Kick	Kick	Kick	Kick	Electric	Electric
PERFORMANCE						
Climbing Ability (deg)	35	35	35	35	N.A.	N.A.
Turning Radius (in)	82.6	82.6	82.6	78.2	N.A.	N.A.
Braking Dist. (ft @ mph)	40 @ 30	40 @ 30	40 @ 30	49 @ 30	N.A.	N.A.
Fuel Consump. (mpg @ mph)	94 @ 25	94 @ 25	94 @ 25	94 @ 31	N.A.	N.A.

① RV—rotary valve; PP—piston port.

② PM—premix; OI—oil injection.

④ Not to be confused with the DTI Enduro. YDTI is a YD3 engine in a YDS2 frame.

   NA—Not available.

⑮ DTIE—245; DT2—258

⑯ DTIE—23 @ 7000; DT2—24 @ 7000

⑰ DTIE—17.5 @ 6500; DT2—18.3 @ 6000

⑱ DTIE—Piston port; DT2—Reed valve

General Specifications, continued

	YDS1	YDS2	Early YDS3	Early YDS3C	Late YDS3	Late YDS3C
DIMENSIONS						
Net Weight (lbs.)	310	310	320	320	320	320
Overall Length (in)	78.3	78.3	79.0	79.0	79.0	79.0
Overall Width (in)	24.2	24.2	31.2	31.2	31.2	31.2
Overall Height (in)	36.6	36.6	42.0	42.0	42.0	42.0
Ground Clearance (in)	5.1	5.1	5.8	5.8	5.8	5.8
Wheelbase (in)	50.8	50.8	51.9	51.9	51.9	51.9
Tire Size (in): front	3.00 x 18	2.75 x 18	3.00 x 18	3.00 x 18	3.00 x 18	3.00 x 18
rear	3.00 x 18	2.75 x 18	3.25 x 18	3.50 x 18	3.25 x 18	3.50 x 18
ENGINE						
Displacement (cc)	246	246	246	246	246	246
No. of Cylinders	2	2	2	2	2	2
Bore X Stroke (mm)	56 x 50	56 x 50	56 x 50	56 x 50	56 x 50	56 x 50
Compression Ratio (:1)	6.8	7.5	7.5	7.8	7.5	7.5
Horsepower @ RPM	N.A.	25 @ 7500	27 @ 8000	27 @ 7500	28 @ 8000	28 @ 8000
Torque @ RPM (ft lbs)	N.A.	17.8 @ 7000	17.6 @ 6500	17.6 @ 6500	18.1 @ 7500	18.1 @ 7500
Fuel Induct. (RV, PP)①	PP	PP	PP	PP	PP	PP
Carburetion (Mikuni)	VM20SC (2)	VM20SH (2)	VM24SC (2)	VM24SC (2)	VM24SC (2)	VM24SC (2)
Lubrication (PM, OI)②	PM	PM	OI	OI	OI	OI
TRANSMISSION						
Clutch	Manual	Manual	Manual	Manual	Manual	Manual
Reduction (pri/sec)	2.500/3.358	3.250/2.438	3.250/2.600	3.250/2.733	3.250/2.600	3.250/2.733
Transmission Ratio: 1st	2.500	2.500	2.500	2.500	2.545	2.545
2nd	1.667	1.667	1.667	1.667	1.533	1.533
3rd	1.227	1.227	1.227	1.227	1.167	1.167
4th	0.960	0.960	0.960	1.042	0.950	0.950
5th	0.750	0.750	0.750	0.923	0.773	0.773
ELECTRICS						
Ignition	Generator	Generator	Generator	Generator	Generator	Generator
Starting	Kick	Kick	Kick	Kick	Kick	Kick
PERFORMANCE						
Climbing Ability (deg)	N.A.	23	23	27	23	27
Turning Radius (in)	N.A.	86.2	88.0	88.0	88	88.0
Braking Dist. (ft @ mph)	N.A.	31 @ 30	47 @ 32	47 @ 32	47 @ 32	47 @ 32
Fuel Consump. (mpg @ mph)	N.A.	100 @ 27	100 @ 25	100 @ 25	100 @ 25	100 @ 25

① RV—rotary valve; PP—piston port.

② PM—premix; OI—oil injection.

NA—Not available.

General Specifications, continued

	YD55	DS6C	QS6B	DS7	YM1	YM2C	YR1
DIMENSIONS							
Net Weight	325.6	309	304	304	340	326	348
Overall Length (in)	78.4	78.3	78.3	—	78.9	73.3	81.2
Overall Width (in)	80.3	32.9	32.9	—	31.2	31.2	28.9
Overall Height (in)	41.4	41.9	41.9	—	42.0	38.1	39.4
Ground Clearance (in)	6.1	5.9	6.1	—	5.9	6.1	5.7
Wheelbase (in)	50.8	50.8	50.8	—	50.7	51.0	52.6
Tire Size (in): front	3.00 x 18	3.00 x 18	3.00 x 18	3.00 x 18	3.00 x 18	3.00 x 18	3.00 x 18
rear	3.25 x 18	3.50 x 18	3.25 x 18	3.25 x 18	3.25 x 18	3.25 x 18	3.50 x 18
ENGINE							
Displacement (cc)	246	246	246	247	305	305	348
No. of Cylinders	2	2	2	2	2	2	2
Bore X Stroke (mm)	56 x 50	56 x 50	56 x 50	54 x 54	60 x 54	60 x 54	61 x 59.6
Compression Ratio (:1)	7.5	7.3	7.3	7.1	6.7	7.5	6.9
Horsepower @ RPM	29.5 @ 8000	30 @ 7500	30 @ 7500	30 @ 7500	29 @ 7000	31 @ 7000	36 @ 7500
Torque @ RPM (ft lbs)	19.7 @ 7500	21.1 @ 7000	21.1 @ 7000	21.1 @ 7000	19.9 @ 6000	23.4 @ 6500	27.8 @ 6500
Fuel Induct. (RV, PP) ①	PP	PP	PP	PP	PP	PP	PP
Carburetion (Mikuni)	VM26SC (2)	VM26SC (2)	VM26SC (2)	VM26SC (2)	VM24SC (2)	VM26SC	VM28SC (2)
Lubrication (PM, OI) ②	OI	OI	OI	OI	OI	OI	OI
TRANSMISSION							
Clutch	Manual	Manual	Manual	Manual	Manual	Manual	Manual
Reduction (pri/sec)	3.250/2.733	3.250/2.929	3.250/2.733	3.238/2.666	3.250/2.353	3.250/2.500	2.870/2.563
Transmission Ratio: 1st	2.545	2.545	2.545	2.562	2.545	2.545	2.545
2nd	1.533	1.533	1.533	1.590	1.533	1.533	1.600
3rd	1.167	1.167	1.167	1.192	1.167	1.167	1.167
4th	0.950	0.950	0.950	0.965	0.950	0.950	0.950
5th	0.773	0.773	0.773	0.806	0.773	0.773	0.773
ELECTRICS							
Ignition	Generator	Generator	Generator	Alternator	Generator	Generator	Generator
Starting	Electric	Kick	Kick	Kick	Kick	Kick	Kick
PERFORMANCE							
Climbing Ability (deg)	23.5	25	24	—	23	23.5	26
Turning Radius (in)	90.7	86.6	86.6	—	88.0	90.6	90.6
Braking Dist. (ft @ mph)	42.5 @ 31	38 @ 31	38 @ 31	—	40 @ 32	42.5 @ 31	43 @ 31
Fuel Consump. (mpg @ mph)	114 @ 35	94 @ 25	94 @ 25	—	82 @ 25	114 @ 35	95 @ 25

① RV—rotary valve; PP—piston port.

② PM—premix; OI—oil injection.

General Specifications, continued

	YR2/YR2C	R3C	R5/R5B/R5C	RT1/RT1B/RT2	XS1/XS1B/XS2
DIMENSIONS					
Net Weight (lbs.)	348	340	308	258	409
Overall Length (in)	81.2	80.3	80.3	82.7	85.4
Overall Width (in)	28.9	35.2	32.9	35.0	35.6
Overall Height (in)	39.4	42.7	42.7	45.7	45.3
Ground Clearance (in)	5.7	5.9	6.1	10.0	5.9
Wheelbase (in)	52.6	52.8	52.0	54.7	55.5
Tire Size (in): front	3.00 x 18	3.00 x 18	3.00 x 18	3.25 x 19	⑲
rear	3.50 x 18	3.50 x 18	3.50 x 18	4.00 x 18	4.00 x 18
ENGINE					
Displacement (cc)	348	348	347	351	653
No. of Cylinders	2	2	2	1	2
Bore X Stroke (mm)	61 x 59.6	61 x 59.6	64 x 54	80 x 70	75 x 74
Compression Ratio (:1)	6.9	7.5	6.9	6.6	⑳
Horsepower @ RPM	36 @ 7000	36 @ 7000	36 @ 7000	㉒	53 @ 7000
Torque @ RPM (ft lbs)	27.8 @ 6000	28 @ 6000	28 @ 6500	㉓	40.1 @ 6000
Fuel Induct. (RV, PP)①	PP	PP	PP	㉔	⑥
Carburetion (Mikuni)	VM28SC (2)	VM28SC (2)	VM28SC (2)	VM32SH	B538
Lubrication (PM, OI)②	OI	OI	OI	OI	⑦
TRANSMISSION					
Clutch	Manual	Manual	Manual	Manual	Manual
Reduction (pri/sec)	2.870/2.563⑤	2.870/2.730	2.869/2.666	3.095/2.600	2.666/2.000
Transmission Ratio: 1st	2.545	2.545	2.562	2.533	㉑
2nd	1.600	1.600	1.590	1.789	1.588
3rd	1.167	1.167	1.192	1.304	1.300
4th	0.950	0.950	0.965	1.000	1.095
5th	0.773	0.773	0.806	0.767	0.956
ELECTRICS					
Ignition	Generator	Generator	Alternator	Magneto	Alternator
Starting	Kick	Kick	Kick	Kick	Kick
PERFORMANCE					
Climbing Ability (deg)	26	26.5	28	35	26
Turning Radius (in)	90.6	90.6	90.6	78.7	98.4
Braking Dist. (ft @ mph)	43 @ 31	43 @ 31	46 @ 31	49 @ 31	46 @ 31
Fuel Consump. (mpg @ mph)	95 @ 25	95 @ 25	82.5 @ 37	82.5 @ 37	82.5 @ 37

① RV—rotary valve; PP—piston port.

② PM—premix; OI—oil injection.

⑤ YR2C—2.870/2.730.

⑥ One exhaust, one intake valve per cylinder.

⑦ Pressure-fed wet sump.

⑲ XS1—3.25 x 19; XS2—3.50 x 19

⑳ XS1—8.7; XS2—8.4

㉑ XS1—2.214; XS2—2.461

㉒ RT1—30 @ 6000; RT2—32 @ 6000

㉓ RT1—26 @ 5500; RT2—27.7 @ 5500

㉔ RT1—Piston port; RT2—Reed valve

2 ● Maintenance

Proper maintenance always pays off in increased reliability and performance, but an extra dividend can be had if you approach the machine's needs with the proper attitude. It's very easy merely to change the oil, adjust the brakes, and ride off. But, if you stay aware and actually take notice of what you're doing, you can gain a sensitivity toward the machine and know BEFOREHAND when something is wearing out or needs attention.

When you encounter a frustrated rider with a seized engine, nine times out of ten he'll tell you that the engine suddenly froze up—just like that! He doesn't mention that the combustion chamber is stuffed with carbon, because he probably isn't aware of it; he may swear to have changed oil and set points, plugs and timing right on schedule, and probably did, but he CERTAINLY never took notice of the engine's subtle changes that would have told him something was going awry.

What it boils down to is preventive maintenance with observation . . . keep to a regular service interval and LOOK at what you're working on. Most likely you'll notice that the chain is wearing down or the clutch cable is becoming frayed, and then be able to replace them BEFORE they break.

Oil Changes and Lubrication

Autolube

Keep a daily check on the Autolube reservoir and refill it as necessary. Don't compromise the engine's life by using a cheap grade—if Yamalube or a good two-stroke oil isn't available, use one of the following:

American	Permalube SAE 30W
Atlantic	Atlantic Aviation SAE 30W
Castrol	Heavy Duty SAE 30W
Gulf	Gulfpride SAE 30W
Humble	ESSO, ENCO, Humble SAE 30W
Kendall	Dual Action, Super Duty SAE 30W
Mobil	Mobil A SAE 30W
Phillips	Sixty-Six SAE 30W
Pure	Super Duty Purelube SAE 30W
Richfield	Richlube Premium SAE 30W
Shell	Shell X-100 SAE 30W
Texaco	Havoline SAE 30W

These are all good down to 18° F or less. If you do much riding in colder weather, use a lighter weight oil SAE 10W/30, but stay with the premium grades.

Two-Stroke Transmission

Drain the oil into a clean container while the engine is hot, then slowly pour it out of the container and look for foreign matter. When you fill the transmission back up again, don't guess at the amount: use a container graduated in cc's or ounces and remember to compensate for oil that's still clinging to the gears. Use a premium grade SAE 10W/30 and once you have selected a brand, stick with it.

XS1/XS2 Engine and Transmission

The XS1/XS2 engine and transmission have a common oil supply. Remove BOTH drain plugs and clean them before reinstallation: they are magnetic and will collect any metallic particles.

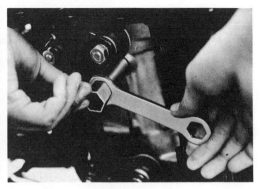

Draining the two-stroke transmission. On earlier twins the drain plug is located at the side of the crankcase, just beneath the case cover.

Also remove and clean the oil filter every oil change and the sump strainer every 10,000 miles.

1. Oil Filter
   a. Remove the attaching Allen screws and the filter cover plate.
   b. Separate the sealing O-ring from the cover plate and inspect it for damage.
   c. Remove the oil filter retaining bolt and pull out the filter.
   d. Clean the filter with solvent and compressed air. Check for damage or any lodged particles in the outer mesh.
   e. Clean out the filter cavity in the crankcase, then reinstall the filter, securing bolt, O-ring, and cover plate.

NOTE: Do not overtighten the retaining bolt because the filter could collapse.

XS1/XS2 oil filter retaining bolt

2. Sump Strainer
   a. Remove the attaching bolts, cover plate, gasket, and strainer.
   b. Clean the strainer with solvent and compressed air.
   c. Reinstall the strainer and cover plate

with a new gasket, then tighten the attaching bolts alternately and snugly.

XS1/XS2 sump strainer retaining bolts

The oil should be changed two or three times during the first 2000 miles and once every 2000 miles, or six months, thereafter. Yamaha recommends a detergent "MS" grade SAE 20W/40 oil for all around riding. The sump capacity is three liters, but refill it with only 2-3/4 liters (5-4/5 pints) to compensate for oil left in delivery passages.

XS1/XS2 drain plugs

After the oil change, set the machine up on its center stand; start and let it run long enough to warm up, then shut it off. After a few minutes, check the dipstick oil level indication.

Grease Fittings

Use a hand gun filled with medium grade grease. This type gun gives complete control over how much grease is fed through the nipple and will ensure a safe pressure.

NOTE: Don't overgrease the rear wheel because the lubricant may get on the brake linings and lessen the machine's stopping power. Remember to grease the often overlooked swing arm fitting.

Final Drive Chain

Make periodic checks and regularly apply commercial chain lubricant. Don't fail to lubricate the chain after a heavy rainfall or when you've been riding through mud. Use a good quality chain lube only, as other types of lubricating grease and oil tend to collect more sand, dust, etc., and don't stick to the chain as well.

In addition to regular service about once every 200 or 300 miles, the chain should be removed and soaked in solvent, well cleaned, then completely dried. This will remove any old grease and dirt that has accumulated between the links. Always wipe the chain clean with rags before applying fresh lubricant.

NOTE: When installing the chain after a solvent soak, make sure the open end of the master link is pointed away from the direction of normal chain rotation.

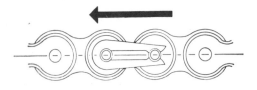

DIRECTION OF TRAVEL

Drive chain master link installation

Front Forks

Change the front fork oil at service intervals or when you want to change the fork's damping qualities.

1. Remove the drain screw at the bottom of each fork leg.

2. Drain the oil, then pump the forks a few times to make sure the tubes are clear.

Front fork oil drain screw

3. Reinstall the screws and remove the fork cap at the top of each leg.

4. Add the proper amount of oil to the inner tube, then reinstall the fork caps and tighten them up snugly.

Front fork cap removal

Under normal conditions, the two-stroke street models should use 10W/30 oil, the trail bikes 10W/30, and the XS1/XS2 30W or 20W (if temperatures are below 40°F). If you want stiffer or softer damping, select an appropriately heavier or lighter viscosity oil.

NOTE: The racing-type forks on the Enduro models are also equipped with an air valve to help adjust damping qualities.

Use a graduated container when refilling the front fork legs

Cables

Lubricate the brake and clutch cable ends with a few drops of engine oil and smear a small amount of light grease on the speedometer, tachometer, and throttle grip cable ends.

Cleaning

Washing and Waxing

Unfortunately, many riders tend to ignore an accumulation of dirt on their machines. This is especially true of trail bikes, which are often run hub-deep in mud or sand. True, the brakes are sealed and the machine is built to take rough treatment, but if you leave the bike sitting in last month's mud, you'll eventually pay the piper. Nothing wears out wheel bearings, chains, and seals faster than dirt. If you want the bike to last, you must treat it right and keep it clean.

The best way to wash the machine is with hot soapy water and a soft-bristled brush. In some instances you may need something stronger, such as commercial grease cutter, to clean the engine area. Don't wash the machine at a commercial high pressure/detergent car wash. The high pressure water and detergent will cut not only through the dirt, but your wheel bearing packings as well!

After the machine is cleaned up and the chain has been lubricated, start it and ride around for about ten minutes. This will warm the engine enough to evaporate any water that has accumulated in vital areas.

Protect painted finishes with automotive-type wax and use chrome polish and preservative on plated surfaces. A good heavy application of these two will not only brighten appearance, but also help prevent corrosion.

Air Cleaner

Wash the air cleaner at least once every two thousand miles (foam type), or blow it out with compressed air every 3000 miles (paper type); more often if you ride dusty roads or trails.

If you have the foam rubber Filtron-type cleaner element, wash it in gasoline or kerosene, then in hot soapy water. Wring out the element and let it dry completely, then place it in a container full of oil. After it is saturated, squeeze out as much oil as possible and then reinstall. This oil/foam air cleaner is the most effective available, IF it is kept clean. Remember that clean air is essential for the engine's

breathing and that, without it, the bike will never reach its performance potential.

Paper air cleaner element removal. The air cleaner is mounted either behind the side cover or directly to the carburetor(s).

Two-Stroke Decarbonization

Normally, heat is dissipated throughout the cylinder head and piston top; if a heavy layer of carbon is present, however, it acts like an insulation blanket and causes all the heat to be concentrated on the rings, plugs, etc. The carbon layer also effectively reduces the combustion chamber displacement and causes significantly higher pressure on the piston and rings. As a result of this increased pressure, and consequent temperature, the rings are more apt to allow blow-by and/or freeze in their grooves, which transfers the heat to the side of the piston. The piston, in turn, swells and burns up its lubrication film, creating more heat. In addition to all this, any blow-by gases contaminating the crankcase and incoming mixture radically upsets the fuel balance, leading to preignition and even GREATER heat.

The decarbonization process is very easy to perform and requires little more time than a four-stroke valve adjustment.

Filtron-type air cleaner element removal. On some models, access to the air cleaner is under the seat.

Removing carbon from the piston crown with a hacksaw blade

1. Remove the cylinder head, cylinder, exhaust pipe, and muffler baffle.

2. Scrape carbon deposits off the cylinder head and piston top, and out of the exhaust port, ring grooves, and exhaust pipe. Use a blunt blade without a point so that you don't scratch any internal surfaces.

Removing carbon from the cylinder head

Cleaning out the piston ring grooves. The piston does not have to be removed for this operation.

Scraping carbon build-up out of the exhaust port

NOTE: Use a broken ring to clean out piston grooves, EXCEPT on models equipped with keystone-type rings. The piston crowns on these machines are stamped with the letter "K".

CAUTION: Be extremely careful in perform-

ing the following operation. Gasoline fumes are highly explosive.

3. Place the baffle in a vise and burn the carbon out with a torch. An alternate, and less safe, procedure is to soak the baffle in gasoline, put it in a safe place (well away from any buildings or flammable material), and set it afire cautiously.

4. LIGHTLY tap the baffle against a wooden block or bench to remove the deposits. Do not beat on the baffle!

Burning carbon deposits with a torch

After everything is cleaned up, put the bike back together and you'll be surprised how much better it runs. Decarbonize when the buildup warrants it, rather than by service intervals. Each machine will vary in its need, but the carbon should be removed at LEAST every 4000 or 5000 miles.

Service Checks and Adjustments

Battery

Check the battery level at least once a month in normal weather and weekly in especially hot weather. Don't take for granted that because the battery is charging, the fluid level is correct. Fill it with distilled water only.

The specific gravity of a fully charged battery is 1.26 to 1.28. If less than this, the battery should be recharged. Also recharge the battery if the machine has been stored for a long period of time.

NOTE: Charging rates and times vary slightly for different models, but never apply more than one ampere to any Yamaha battery. While charging, the fluid level may drop; this is normal, so fill it as necessary.

Nuts and Bolts

Whenever you're working on the machine, tighten up any loose external nuts and bolts.

Tapping the exhaust baffle

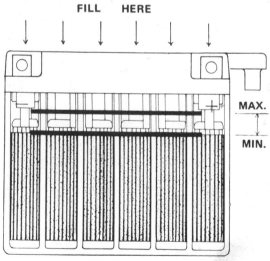

Battery fluid level is OK if it is between the minimum
and maximum lines marked on the battery

Use the proper metric wrenches; they provide
the correct angle and amount of leverage. Don't
overtighten, but make sure everything is snug.
Focus special attention on the following:

1. Front and rear axle nuts.
2. Swing arm shaft nuts.
3. Footrests and brake pedal.
4. Center and side stands.
5. Muffler mounting bolts.
6. Engine mounting bolts.
7. Wheel spokes.
8. Any points subject to vibration or road
shock.

Tire Pressure

Tire pressure is one of the main factors affect-
ing safety and handling. The factory pressures
are fine to start with, but you may adjust them

to your weight and the type of riding you do.
Keep in mind that the pressure will rise as the
temperature of the tire increases, but don't
underinflate! It has been found that riding on
tires inflated 5 psi below normal at 60 mph is
equivalent in heat buildup to riding on normally inflated tires at 80 mph.

NOTE: It's a good idea to invest in an accurate tire gauge; gas station air pump gauges
are often inaccurate.

Cables

Make certain that all cables operate freely and
that their sleeves are not binding anywhere on
the bike; check especially under the gas tank.
Also make sure that all cable spring-returns
function properly and that the adjuster wheel
slots aim down or back (this will prevent water
from entering the cable sleeves).

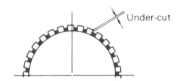

The arrows indicate the mica undercut. See Electrical
Systems for wear limits.

Removing brush dust from the mica undercut

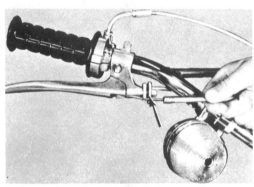

After checking cable condition, turn the adjuster
wheel so that the slot (indicated by arrow) is pointing
downward

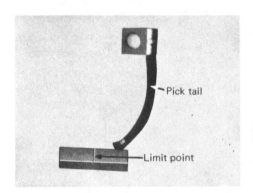

Brush wear limits are usually indicated by a line drawn
on the brush. Also see Electrical Systems.

Generator Brushes

Begin regular inspection after 4000 miles.
Dust from the generator brushes tends to collect on the mica undercut, so if necessary, polish up the commutator surface with emery
cloth and remove any collected dust with a
knife or screwdriver blade.

Brakes

Inspection

Remove the wheels periodically and check
the shoes and drums for excessive wear or glaz-

Polishing the generator commutator

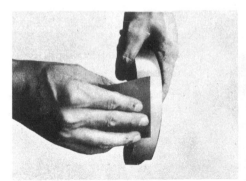

Removing brake shoe surface glaze. See Chassis Chapter for brake lining wear limits.

ing. Grease or oil on the linings will cause poor stopping power; dirt or uneven wear will cause squealing. Remove any surface glaze with fine sandpaper or emery cloth. Replace the linings if they are excessively worn or show any signs of oil penetration.

Adjustment

Yamaha twin leading-shoe type front brakes normally grab quickly and don't require much lever pressure. If the lever feels soft or spongy, chances are that both shoes aren't making contact at the same time. To correct this condition or after installing new shoes:

1. Disconnect the brake cable at the hand lever.

2. Loosen the locknut on the rod between the cam operating arms (see illustration).

Arrow indicates the front brake cam operating rod locknut

3. Turn the rod so that the operating arms spread apart enough to take up all slack, but no more.

4. Tighten the locknut.

5. Connect the cable back to the lever, then spin the wheel and turn the cable adjuster. Listen at the drum and you should hear both shoes make contact at the same time. If they don't, readjust the rod and check again.

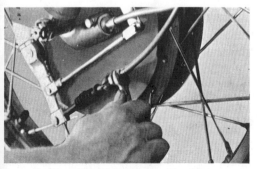

Backing off the front brake cable adjuster

6. When the shoes are set correctly, backoff the adjuster until you have 1/4 in. of slack in the cable.

7. Make the final adjustment at the hand lever to suit the rider, but keep the lever-to-bracket gap at around 1/8 in.

Adjust the rear brake at the rod (or cable) end to obtain approximately 1 in. pedal freeplay. Make this adjustment at regular intervals with the front brake and anytime the rear wheel is removed or the chain adjusted.

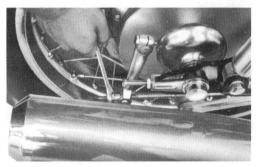

Rear brake adjustment

NOTE: Don't set brake clearances too close when cold; linings may drag and become glazed when warm.

Disc Brake Adjustment

The 1972 XS2 is equipped with a hydraulic front disc brake. Adjustment is performed at the handlever, where there should be 1/2 to 1 in. freeplay. Turn the adjusting screw until this clearance is obtained between the handlever and the actuating piston.

Stoplight Switch

Late model Yamahas are equipped with two switches so that application of either the front or rear brake will actuate the stoplight. The rear switch is mounted in a slotted bracket to provide a means of adjustment. Set the switch position so that actuation occurs just before the brake shoes make contact.

Clutch

Check the clutch adjustment periodically or whenever the clutch slips or grabs. There are two points of adjustment and they should be set in proper order:

1. Clutch pushrod

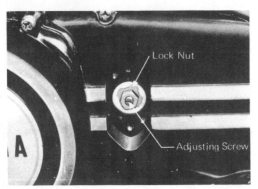

Clutch pushrod adjustment through case cover access hole

a. Remove the access plug on the clutch housing.

NOTE: On some models, the righthand case cover must be removed.

Clutch pushrod adjustment with case cover removed

b. Loosen the pushrod setscrew locknut.
c. Turn the setscrew IN until it bottoms against the pushrod, then back it OUT one-quarter turn.
d. Tighten the locknut and reinstall the access plug or case cover.
2. Clutch cable
Set the lever-to-bracket clearance at 1/8 in. by loosening the locknut, turning the adjuster

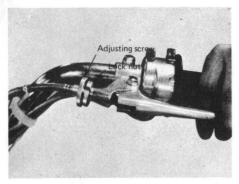

Clutch cable adjustment at the hand lever

wheel for the correct gap, then retightening the locknut.

NOTE: On some models, the clutch cable adjustment is made at the other end of the cable, where it enters the crankcase or case cover.

Clutch cable adjustment at the case cover

Chain

Keep a constant check on the chain tension. Measure freeplay with a rider on the bike, but only one foot touching the ground for balance. Total up-and-down movement of the chain should be approximately 1/2–3/4 in.; more if you ride two-up often.

To adjust the chain:

1. Remove the cotter pin and loosen the rear axle nut.
2. Loosen the chain adjuster locknut on each side.
3. Turn both adjuster bolts an EQUAL amount to achieve correct freeplay. Make certain the alignment marks on the swing arm ends are the same to ensure correct rear wheel positioning.

1 Rear axle nut   3 Adjuster bolt
2 Adjuster locknut   4 Alignment marks

4. Tighten the adjuster bolt locknuts, then tighten the rear axle nut and install a new cotter key.

Also check the chain, countershaft sprocket and rear wheel sprocket for signs of wear. Remember that these three components will transfer wear to one another: an excessively worn rear sprocket will prematurely wear out the chain, which will quickly wear out the countershaft sprocket, etc. Don't forget to adjust the rear brake and stoplight switch whenever you adjust the chain.

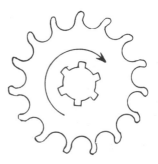

Sprocket with wear spots

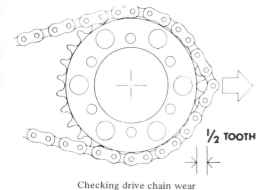

Checking drive chain wear

Unworn sprocket

Checking countershaft sprocket wear

Storage

Before Storing

If the bike is to be stored for a period of two months or more, follow this procedure to ensure minimum deterioration:

1. Wash the bike thoroughly, then ride it at least fifteen minutes to evaporate any moisture accumulated in and around the engine. Make sure the bike is COMPLETELY dry.

2. Drain the oil (two-stroke transmission, XS1/XS2 sump) and refill it to the proper level with fresh SAE 20W/40 (XS1/XS2) or SAE 10W/30 (two-strokes).

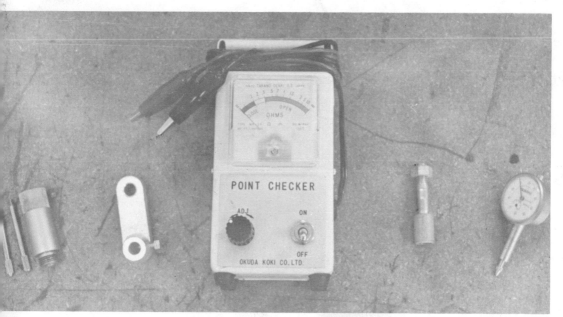

Two-stroke tune-up tools

3. Run the engine for ten or fifteen minutes to circulate the new lubricant, then turn off the fuel petcock; just before the engine stops, squirt some oil into the carburetor throat(s) to help prevent the pistons, cylinders and rings from rusting.

4. If storing for two months or less, leave the gas tank full; for longer periods of time, drain the tank and add 1/2 cup of oil to a quart of gasoline; shake the bike vigorously to coat the tank walls.

NOTE: Keep in mind that fuel or fumes in the tank could be a fire hazard.

5. Make sure the battery is fully charged before storing it and lubricate the terminal connections with a heavy coat of grease. Recharge the battery every two months to keep it alive. If the bike's storage location is rather dry or hot, remove the battery and store it in a cool basement.

6. Disconnect the fuel lines at the carburetor(s) and seal the openings tightly.

7. Lubricate all points: grease fittings, cable ends, chain, etc.

8. Apply a heavy coat of wax on all painted, chromed and polished surfaces. Grease offers more chrome protection, but makes for quite a clean up job.

9. Set the machine up on its center stand (or block it up), then throw over a protective canvas cover.

After Storing

When taking the bike out of storage, go over it completely, checking all points of maintenance: plugs, points, timing, valve adjustment (XS1/XS2), battery charge, brakes, etc. Also inspect the carburetor and fuel petcock for any gum deposits. Disassemble and clean, if necessary. Always replace old fuel in the tank and check for any evidence of rusting. When connecting the battery terminals, remember that Yamaha batteries are all NEGATIVE ground. Don't forget to check the tire pressures before riding off into that sunny spring day.

Periodic Maintenance
(After First 3000 Miles)

These are normal service intervals. In cases of hard use, maintenance should be performed more often.

Daily (before each riding)
Check Autolube reservoir
Check tire pressures
Check chain freeplay
Check cables
Check brake operation
Check clutch operation

Weekly (in hot weather)
Check battery fluid level

Monthly (in normal weather)
Check battery fluid level

Bi-Monthly
Charge stored battery

Every 200 miles
Lubricate chain
Check hydraulic brake reservoir

Every 2000 miles
Change gearbox oil (two-strokes)
Change sump oil (XS1/XS2)
Clean oil filter (XS1/XS2)
Lubricate grease fittings
Lubricate cables
Soak chain in solvent
Adjust brakes
Adjust clutch
Tighten nuts and bolts
Wash Filtron air cleaner
Perform complete tune-up

Every 3000 miles
Replace paper air cleaner

Every 4000 miles
Change front fork oil
De-carbonize two-strokes
Check generator brushes
Check brake linings
Clean carburetors

Every 10,000 miles
Clean sump strainer (XS1/XS2)

Maintenance Data

	Fuel Tank Capacity (Gal)	Autolube Oil Capacity (Qt)	Gearbox [XS1 Sump] Oil Capacity (Qt)	Front Fork① Oil Capacity (cc) (oz)		Chain Freeplay (in)	Tire Pressure Front/Rear (psi)
U5, U5L, U5E	0.90	1.60	0.50	—	—	$^1/_2-^5/_8$	$^{22}/_{28}$
U7E	1.20	1.50	0.65	—	—	$^{25}/_{32}$	$^{20}/_{28}$
MJ2, MJ2T	0.90	—	0.50	130	4.4	$^1/_2-^5/_8$	$^{22}/_{28}$
YJ1	1.38	—	0.50	—	—	$^1/_2-^5/_8$	$^{22}/_{28}$
YJ2	1.38	1.16	0.50	130	4.4	$^1/_2-^5/_8$	$^{22}/_{28}$
JT1, JT2L, JT2M	1.10	1.10	0.64	②		$^{25}/_{32}$	$^{22}/_{28}$
MG1, MG1T	0.90	—	0.50	130	4.4	$^1/_2-^5/_8$	$^{22}/_{28}$
YG1, YG1T	1.72	—	0.50	130	4.4	$^1/_2-^5/_8$	$^{22}/_{28}$
YG1K, YG1TK, YGS1, YGS1T	1.72	1.15	0.50	130	4.4	$^1/_2-^5/_8$	$^{22}/_{28}$
YG5T	1.60	1.48	0.65	140	4.7	$^1/_2-^5/_8$	$^{25}/_{27}$
G5S	1.60	1.50	0.65	③		$^{25}/_{32}$	$^{26}/_{28}$
G6S	1.60	1.50	0.65	130	4.4	$^{25}/_{32}$	$^{26}/_{28}$
G6SB, GTS	1.60	1.50	0.65	③		$^{25}/_{32}$	$^{20}/_{28}$
HT1, HT1B	1.70	1.30	0.75	140	4.7	$^{25}/_{32}$	$^{14}/_{17}$
HS1, HS1B, LS2	2.00	④	0.85	147	5.0	$^{25}/_{32}$	$^{20}/_{28}$
YL2, YL2C, YL2CM	2.20	1.70	0.75	145	4.9	$^1/_2-^5/_8$	$^{25}/_{27}$
L5T, L5TA	1.80	1.50	0.65	140	4.7	$^{25}/_{32}$	$^{26}/_{28}$
LT2	1.60	1.30	0.75	136	4.6	$^{25}/_{32}$	$^{14}/_{17}$
YL1, YL1E	1.95	1.16	0.75	130	4.4	$^1/_2-^5/_8$	$^{25}/_{27}$
YA5	2.27	—	1.05	180	6.1	$^5/_8-^3/_4$	$^{22}/_{28}$
YA6	2.38	1.90	1.40	170	5.8	$^5/_8-^3/_4$	$^{22}/_{28}$
AT1, AT1B, AT1C, AT2	1.89	1.27	0.78	⑤		$^{25}/_{32}$	$^{14}/_{17}$
YAS1, YAS1C	2.50	1.59	0.85	160	5.4	$^1/_2-^5/_8$	$^{25}/_{27}$
AS2C	2.00	1.59	0.85	160	5.4	$^{25}/_{32}$	$^{26}/_{28}$
CT1, CT1B, CT1C, CT2	1.89	1.27	0.78	⑤		$^{25}/_{32}$	$^{14}/_{17}$
YCS1	3.4	2.1	0.85	170	5.8	$^{25}/_{32}$	$^{26}/_{28}$
YCS1C	3.0	2.0	0.85	170	5.8	$^{25}/_{32}$	$^{26}/_{28}$
CS3C, CS3B, CS5	2.4	2.0	0.85	⑤		$^{25}/_{32}$	$^{26}/_{28}$
DT1, DT1B, DT1C	2.5	1.7	1.06	210	7.1	$^{25}/_{32}$	$^{14}/_{17}$
DT1E	2.5	1.7	1.06	175	5.9	$^{25}/_{32}$	$^{13}/_{16}$
YD3	3.2	—	1.25	200	6.7	$^5/_8-^3/_4$	$^{22}/_{28}$
YDT1	4.13	—	1.25	200	6.7	$^5/_8-^3/_4$	$^{22}/_{28}$
YDS1, YDS2	4.13	—	1.50	200	6.7	$^5/_8-^3/_4$	$^{22}/_{28}$
Early YDS3, YDS3C	3.70	1.70	1.50	200	6.7	$^5/_8-^3/_4$	$^{22}/_{28}$
Late YDS3, YDS3C	3.70	1.70	1.75	200	6.7	$^5/_8-^3/_4$	$^{22}/_{28}$
YDS5	4.00	2.50	1.75	200	6.7	$^5/_8-^3/_4$	$^{22}/_{28}$
DS6, DS6C, DS6B	2.90	1.60	1.75	200	6.7	$^{25}/_{32}$	$^{26}/_{28}$
YM1	3.70	1.70	1.75	200	6.7	$^5/_8-^3/_4$	$^{22}/_{28}$
YM2C	4.00	2.50	1.75	200	6.7	$^5/_8-^3/_4$	$^{22}/_{28}$
YR1	4.50	3.25	1.27	240	8.1	$^5/_8-^3/_4$	$^{22}/_{28}$
YR2, YR2C	3.80	3.40	1.27	240	8.1	$^5/_8-^3/_4$	$^{22}/_{28}$
R3C	4.00	3.40	1.27	240	8.1	$^{25}/_{32}$	$^{23}/_{28}$
R5, RSB, R5C, DS7	3.20	2.10	1.60	145	4.9	$^{25}/_{32}$	$^{22}/_{28}$
RT1	2.50	1.70	1.06	210	7.1	$^{25}/_{32}$	$^{20}/_{24}$
RT1B, RT2	2.50	1.70	1.06	175	5.9	$^{25}/_{32}$	$^{13}/_{16}$
XS1, XS1B, XS2	3.30	—	3.20	⑥		$^{25}/_{32}$	$^{23}/_{28}$

① Each leg

② Right leg—97cc (3.3 oz), left leg—120cc (4.1 oz)

③ Right leg—154cc (5.2 oz), left leg—136cc (4.6 oz)

④ HS1—1.6; LS2—1.5

⑤ AT1/CT1—150cc (5.1 oz.); AT2/CT2—120cc (4.1 oz.)

⑥ XS1—240cc (8.1 oz.); XS2—135cc (4.6 oz.)

3 ● Tune-Up

Two-Stroke Tuning

Tuning the two-stroke engine is only a matter of setting ignition points, plugs, timing, carburetion, oil pump stroke, and cable clearances. Keep in mind, however, that while the procedures are both quick and simple, two-stroke engine design inherently makes each adjustment critical.

Should you want to delve into speed tuning, refer to Chapter Nine, Performance and Racing Modifications, but keep in mind that more tools, greater skill and an infinite amount of patience will be required. Unless you need special engine output characteristics for racing, it is recommended to adhere to the factory tuning specifications.

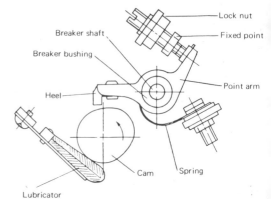

Typical breaker point arrangement on magneto models

ted surfaces, then apply lacquer thinner or point cleaner.

Ignition Points and Timing

1. Remove the ignition access cover, then separate the points and check their condition. Blueing and slight pitting are signs of normal wear; built-up mounds and matching depressions require point set replacement. It is also a good idea to replace the points if you can't remember when you installed the present set.

2. Clean up a used set of points by running a point file or piece of sand paper between them. Remove any deposits and smooth out the pit-

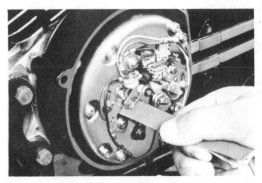

Cleaning the breaker points

NOTE: Apply thinner or cleaner to a new set of points as well, since many of them are coated with a protective film.

3. Snap the points shut on a white business card (or piece of heavy paper) to remove the filings and cleaning fluid. Repeat this step until the points leave a clean imprint.

Removing the point cleaner fluid

4. Remove the spark plug and rotate the engine until the points are at their widest gap.

5. Insert the proper size feeler gauge, loosen the point lockscrew and adjust the gap until a snug slip fit is obtained. Tighten the lockscrew and recheck the gap.

6. Apply a small amount of grease to the point cam or, if equipped with a felt lubricator, a few drops of lightweight oil to the pad.

Checking breaker point gap

7. Before setting the ignition timing, note the following:

a. On models equipped with a governor or electric starter, wedge the centrifugal coun-

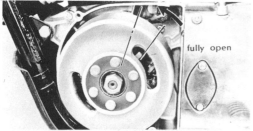
RT1 governor wedged fully open

terweights in the OPEN position. Wooden matchsticks or a piece of wheel spoke (bent into a U-shaped spring) will do the job.

b. On magneto equipped models, ignition timing is determined by the point gap. After the gap has been set, connect the dial indicator and timing light as described below, then readjust the points so that they open at EXACTLY the correct mark. On models equipped with an alternator or generator, point gap and ignition timing are set independently.

c. On twins, each point set is gapped and timed separately. Follow the procedure for each cylinder.

8. Install a dial indicator gauge and adapter in the spark plug opening.

Dial indicator installation on all models except DT1 and RT1

NOTE: DT1 and RT1 cylinder heads must be removed to facilitate the installation of the dial gauge and a special adapter (see illustration).

Dial indicator and special adapter installation on the DT1 and RT1

9. Rotate the crankshaft until the piston reaches top dead center (where the indicator needle stops before reversing direction). Set the dial gauge at zero.

10. Connect a low resistance (100 ohms or less) ignition test lamp or Yamaha Point Checker as follows:

(+) RED lead—to connector on insulated
  side of point set.
(-) BLACK lead—to ground
  (engine case or frame).
NOTE: On twins, the right cylinder points
can be identified by the I_1 terminal (grey
wire) and the left cylinder points by the I_2
terminal (orange wire).

11. Loosen the breaker plate lockscrew just
enough to allow SLIGHT movement (this is a
precaution against any change in plate position
when the lockscrew is retightened).

12. Turn the crankshaft in the direction OP-
POSITE of normal rotation to a point somewhere below the timing mark, then reverse
direction and slowly approach the specified
number of degrees before TDC. Adjust the
breaker plate so that the points just begin to
open (as indicated by the test lamp) at this
mark.

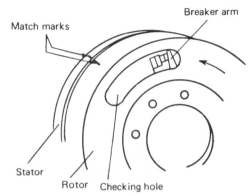

Emergency point gap and timing adjustment on magneto equipped models

13. Tighten the breaker plate lockscrew and
recheck the timing. Readjust if necessary.

In a situation where only a feeler gauge is
available, you can make a rough adjustment
that is reasonably accurate. On magneto sys-

Adjusting ignition timing

NOTE: Turning the breaker plate in the direction of normal engine rotation retards timing; turning opposite to normal rotation ad-
vances timing.

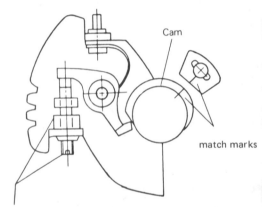

Adjustment should be made with this nut and
screw, when the heel is on the cam lobe.

Timing mark alignment on single-cylinder generator
equipped models

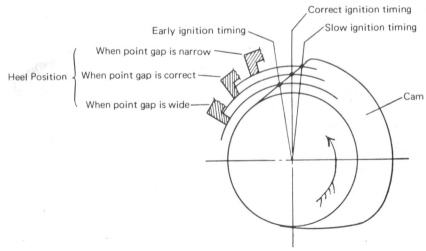

Relationship between breaker point heel, cam and ignition timing

tems, simply adjust the points to the specified gap (this will closely approximate the correct timing); on alternator or dc generator systems, adjust the points, hold a piece of thin cellophane between them, then turn the engine in the direction of normal rotation while tugging lightly at the cellophane—the points should release the cellophane just as the timing marks on the flywheel and breaker plate match.

Spark Plugs

Cleaning and Gapping

Sandblasting is the best method of cleaning plugs: it is very quick, very thorough, and your local gas station is more than likely equipped to do the job. Every motorcycle rider should carry extra plugs, so there needn't be any great inconvenience in leaving a couple to be cleaned.

Check and set the spark plug gap with a wire feeler gauge. Most gauges are equipped with a little notch in the handle for bending the ground electrode to the correct clearance.

Gap measurement is made between the ground and positive electrodes

NOTE: It's a good idea to install new spark plugs at tune-up intervals and keep the most recent (if they are in good condition) as spares. In the long run, new plugs every 2000 miles will prove economical (better gas mileage, lower oil consumption, etc.).

Replacement

There are several important points to keep in mind when replacing plugs:

1. NGK spark plugs are designed specifically to suit the needs of Yamaha two-stroke engines and they should be used whenever possible.

2. Make certain that you get the correct reach plug. The letter H in NGK plug designations indicates a 1/2 in. reach; the letter E indicates a 3/4 in. reach. Installing the wrong one will bring about either plug fouling or eventual (if not immediate) engine damage: too short a reach causes rapid carbon buildup; too long a reach causes excessive heat concentration on the piston crown or, in some cases, causes the piston to hit the plug electrode on each stroke (of which there wouldn't be very many.)

3. All Yamahas use a 14 mm thread spark plug.

4. When installing either new or used plugs, make certain to use a plug wrench ONLY and remember to torque the plug to specifications. Using any tool other than a plug wrench can easily strip the threads in an aluminum cylinder head, and failing to torque the plug will inhibit its ability to dissipate heat. 22-25 ft. lbs. is correct value for all 14 mm plugs. Don't over torque!

Carburetor Idle Speed and Mixture

1. Turn the idle mixture (air) screw IN until it seats lightly.

CAUTION: Too much pressure when turning in the adjustment screw will damage the seat.

2. Back out the idle mixture (air) screw the recommended number of turns.

3. Start and warm up the engine; then, with

Throttle Stop

Air Screw

Throttle stop and air screw location on early piston port engines

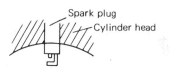

(Too long)
Overheating

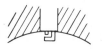

(Proper)

(Too short)
Carbon build-up
results in a sooty
spark plug

Make sure you install the correct reach spark plug

the throttle grip completely closed, turn the idle speed (throttle stop) screw in or out until the engine idles at the specified rpm.

Throttle stop and air screw location on late piston port engines

NOTE: On twins, you can check idle speed synchronization by holding one hand behind each muffler and noting the exhaust pulse frequency. Reset the idle speed screws until the cylinders are firing alternately and at the same rate. If one side is backfiring or its pulses are erratic, stop the engine; turn both idle speed screws IN until lightly seated, then turn them back OUT EQUALLY a couple of turns (enough to prevent stalling). Start the engine and turn either cylinder's idle speed

Throttle stop adjustment on rotary valve engines

Air screw adjustment on rotary valve engines

screw IN, then OUT, and note any increase or decrease in engine speed. At the position where 1/2-to-1 turn does not cause a variation in rpm, the cylinders should be firing smoothly and at the same rate. The idle rpm may be higher than specified, but by equally backing out both idle mixture screws, you can lower it to normal.

Twin Carburetor Synchronization

After setting ignition timing, points, plugs, idle speed, and mixture, you also must synchronize the carburetor slides.

1. Make certain the carburetor bodies are level and parallel to each other by viewing the float bowl joining gasket from the side and rear.

2. If the bodies are misaligned, loosen the carburetor mounts and starter jet linkage. Reposition the bodies correctly and tighten the mounting clamp screws, then check the starter jet linkage to make certain that some freeplay exists and that both jets will close fully.

3. Remove the carburetor/air cleaner elbow(s).

4. Twist the throttle grip fully open to lift up the slides.

5. Position a mirror behind the carburetors or reach into both carburetor bores with the fingers of your free hand.

6. Slowly close the throttle grip and watch or feel the slides as they are being lowered: both should enter their carburetor bores simultaneously.

7. If the slide positions are unequal, raise or lower one to match the other by turning the cable end adjuster at the top of the carburetor.

Throttle Cable Adjustment

Proper adjustment is an important factor in extending cable life, ensuring proper actuation and reducing the possibility of a failure. On most models, a cable runs from the twist grip to a junction block, and from the junction block, one or more cables are routed to the carburetor(s). One end of each cable is fitted with an adjustment nut, located at the twist grip cable guide or the carburetor top(s).

After setting the specified freeplay at each cable separately, start and warm up the engine, then turn the handlebars from side to side and note any change in idle rpm. If a variation occurs, one of the cables is either adjusted incorrectly (not enough freeplay) or is binding somewhere along its routing.

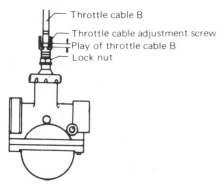

Typical throttle cable arrangement at the carburetor top

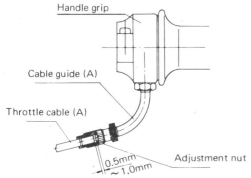

Typical throttle cable arrangement at the twist grip (piston port engines)

Oil Pump Cable Adjustment

NOTE: Before making this critical adjustment, the throttle cables MUST be set correctly.

1. Remove the oil pump access cover.
2. Slowly turn the twist grip to the specified throttle slide opening. "Idle" position is where all cable freeplay is removed, but before the throttle slide begins to lift. "1/2" position is

Half open throttle slide position

where the mark on the throttle slide is at the top of the slide bore.

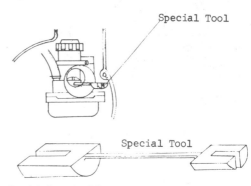

Special throttle slide tool used on early rotary valve models

NOTE: Some early models don't have the "1/2" throttle slide mark. On these machines, use the special pump setting tool (see illustration).

3. Loosen the oil pump cable adjuster locknut.
4. Turn the cable adjuster until the mark on the cable pulley matches the pump guide pin.
5. Tighten the cable locknut.

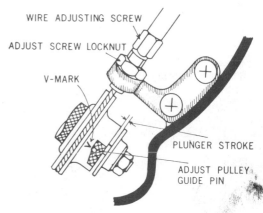

Single-cylinder engine oil pump adjustment marks

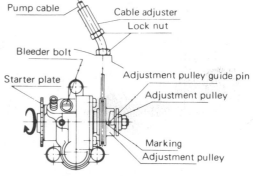

Twin-cylinder engine oil pump alignment marks

Minimum Oil Pump Stroke

1. With the engine stopped, fully close the throttle twist grip.

2. Turn the oil pump starter plate in the direction of the arrow marked on the plate until the plunger is at the end of its stroke.

Oil pump minimum stroke adjustment

3. Using a feeler gauge, measure the clearance between the adjusting pulley and adjusting plate.

4. If the clearance is not within specifications, remove the adjusting plate and add or subtract 0.1 mm shims as necessary.

Add as many shims as necessary to achieve correct minimum stroke

XS1/XS2 Tuning

The XS1/XS2 has a rather sophisticated power-plant incorporating a chain-driven overhead camshaft, alternator ignition, and SU-type constant-vacuum carburetors. Tuning the engine, however, is straightforward and, once mastered, quite simple.

Cam Chain Tensioner

The first item that has to be adjusted is the cam chain tensioner, which is located between the cylinders at the rear of the engine. It consists of a spring-loaded wheel and pushrod assembly that exerts a constant pressure against the chain and takes up any slack. During tune-ups, an adjustment must be made to compensate for normal chain wear in order to ensure accurate piston position readings for setting ignition timing and valve clearances.

Cam chain tensioner housing bolts

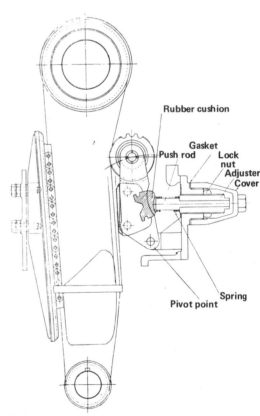

Cross section of cam chain tensioner

1. Remove the four 6 mm attaching bolts and the tensioner housing.

2. Rotate the crankshaft counterclockwise (viewing from the left side of the engine) to position all chain slack at the tensioner.

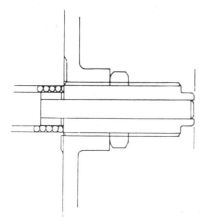

Tensioner correct

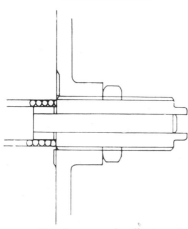

Tensioner needs adjustment

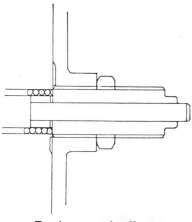

Tensioner needs adjustment

Cam chain tensioner adjustment

3. Remove the protective cover and loosen the tensioner locknut.

4. Using a 22 mm wrench, turn the adjuster IN until the pushrod end is flush with the adjuster (see illustration).

5. Tighten the tensioner locknut.

Ignition Points and Timing

1. Remove the alternator inspection plate, ignition points cover, and centrifugal advance unit cover.

2. Inspect, clean and gap the points as described in two-stroke tuning.

3. Ignition timing is set by matching the marks on the alternator stator and rotor. The rotor has one reference timing mark and the stator has four: the first mark (to right of the letter T) identifies Top Dead Center, the next two marks (either side of the letter F) identify idle timing (fully retarded) and the remaining mark identifies high speed timing (fully advanced).

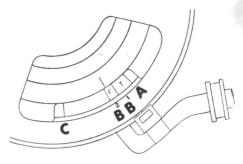

A-Top Dead Center

B^1 & B^2—Ignition Fire Marks

C-Mark for "Fully Advanced" Ignition
   Timing

   XS1/XS2 rotor and stator timing marks

4. Secure the centrifugal advance counterweights in the fully retarded idle position (held inward).

5. Connect an ignition timing light or Yamaha Point Checker as follows:

   (+) RED lead—to grey point wire connector

   (−) BLACK lead—to ground (frame or engine case)

Right and left cylinder point sets are marked R (grey wire) and L (orange wire).

NOTE: The right cylinder timing MUST be set first. The right cylinder points are mounted directly to the base plate, the left cylinder points are mounted on a separate plate; therefore, setting the left side first would cause a position shift when timing the right.

Right and left cylinder points are identified by letters stamped in the base plate

6. Turn the crankshaft in the direction of normal rotation until the right cylinder points begin to open (as indicated by the timing light or Yamaha Point Checker).

7. Make the necessary plate adjustment so that the points begin to open when the rotor mark is aligned with the letter F.

NOTE: On engines with serial numbers below 11764, align the rotor with the mark to the left of the letter F.

8. Switch the (+) RED lead to the orange point wire connector and repeat the procedure for the left cylinder.

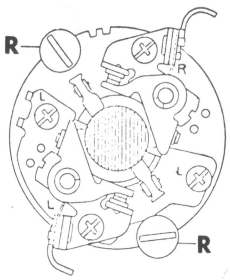

Base plate setscrews

9. After idle timing has been set on both cylinders, secure the centrifugal advance counterweights in the fully advanced (held outward) position: the points should open at the high speed stator mark or just after the mark on engines with serial numbers below 11764. Make any necessary adjustments and recheck the idle timing.

Spark Plugs

Service the spark plugs as described in two-stroke tuning. The XS1/XS2 uses a 3/4 in. reach spark plug.

Valve Clearance

1. Remove valve tappet and alternator covers.

2. Position one cylinder at TDC by aligning the rotor reference mark with the first stator mark. The cylinder at TDC can be identified by slack at both valve adjusters.

3. Insert the specified size feeler gauge between the valve stem and tappet.

4. If adjustment is necessary to achieve a slip fit, loosen the adjuster locknut and turn the adjuster in or out until the correct clearance is obtained.

5. Hold the adjuster securely and tighten the locknut.

6. Rotate the crankshaft 360° and realign the rotor and stator marks, then repeat the procedure on the other cylinder.

Carburetor Idle Speed and Mixture

1. Turn both idle mixture screws IN until lightly seated, then back them OUT 1/2 turn.

2. Adjust both idle speed screws so that the engine idles fast.

3. Disconnect either spark plug lead and back OUT the running cylinder's idle speed screw until the engine dies, then restart the engine and repeat this step on the other cylinder.

4. The engine should now idle smoothly. If the rpm is too high, turn both idle speed screws EQUALLY IN until it falls within specifications.

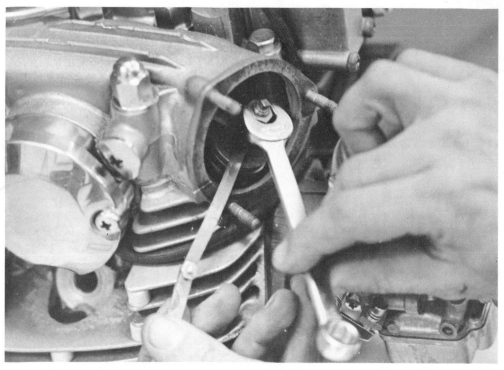

XS1/XS2 valve adjustment

1 Idle mixture screw   2 Throttle stop screw

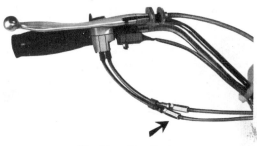

Throttle cable adjusters

Carburetor Synchronization

Both butterfly valves must open simultaneously for the engine to pull smoothly and evenly.
   NOTE: Idle speed MUST be set correctly before synchronizing the carburetors.
   1. Fully close the throttle twist grip.
   2. Slowly open the twist grip and note when the butterfly actuator mechanisms lift off their throttle stop screws.
   3. If they don't lift off simultaneously, shorten or lengthen either cable until they do. The cable adjusters are located about 8 in. below the throttle twist grip.

Throttle Cable Adjustment

With the twist grip fully closed, set both throttle cables so that they have approximately 1.0 mm freeplay before the butterfly valves begin to open.

Tune-up Analysis

The factory equips each model with standard spark plugs and carburetor jets. The values of these items, however, are not necessarily the best for every machine. Ignition spark and carburetion requirements vary with atomospheric conditions and riding habits. In many cases, the engine runs poorly with the standard plugs and jets. The easiest method of determining what changes (if any) should be made, involves removing the spark plug(s) and reading their appearance and condition.

To enable you to make accurate interpretations, the engine MUST first be in perfect tune and mustn't be suffering from any internal mechanical ills. Bad rings or leaking carburetors, valves (XS1/XS2), seals, etc. will cause erroneous readings and will lead you to the wrong conclusions.

Spark Plug Readings

1. After a complete tune-up and installing new plugs, take the machine out and ride it as you normally would.

NOTE: If this isn't feasible, set the bike up on its centerstand or some boxes and run the engine UNDER LOAD at approximately your normal throttle opening (most often used).

2. After at least ten minutes of highway cruising, riding around the block, rock bashing or standing in the driveway holding the throttle open, shut the engine off IMMEDIATELY. Don't let it idle or turn over under compression.

3. Remove the spark plug(s) and inspect the insulating porcelain around the positive electrode:

a. White in color—plug is too hot or fuel mixture is too lean.

b. Blistered—plug is too hot or fuel mixture is too lean.

c. Tan in color—this indicates CORRECT plug heat range and mixture.

d. Dark brown in color—plug is too cold or fuel mixture is too rich.

e. Oily—plug is too cold or oil mixture is too rich.

f. Black in color—plug is too cold, fuel mixture is too rich, or carbon build-up is excessive.

g. Plug condition should be almost identical on twins.

Spark Plug Heat Range

Although spark plugs are available in various heat ranges, this rating doesn't necessarily indicate that they operate at different temperatures. On the contrary, most plugs are designated to maintain approximately 450-850° C under different ENGINE operating temperatures. If the nose (tip) temperature drops below 450° C, the electrode will foul with carbon deposits (especially in two-strokes); if it rises above 850° C, preignition and possible engine damage will occur.

If your plug readings were only slightly abnormal, changing to a one-step hotter or one-step colder spark plug should be all that is necessary. When one step is insufficient, some carburetor mixture changes should also be made.

	NGK
Hotter type ↑	B—7H
	B—7HZ
	B—8H
↓ Colder type	B—8HC
	B—9HC

NGK plug heat range is indicated by the number in its designation. The larger the number, the colder the plug.

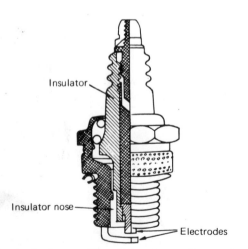

Insulator

Insulator nose

Electrodes

Spark plug construction. Make plug readings at the insulator nose.

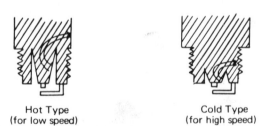

Hot Type (for low speed)   Cold Type (for high speed)

The area of the insulator exposed to combustion, and its radiation distance to the cylinder head, determines spark plug heat range

Carburetor Mixture Adjustment

The fuel/air mixture can be altered at the needle jet and the main jet. The jet needle is adjusted by repositioning its clip in a different groove and the main jet by replacing it with a different size.

If the plug reading indicated too rich a mixture, install a one-step smaller main jet; if it indicated too lean a mixture, install a one-step larger main jet. Should more than a one-size main jet change be needed, you should also reposition the jet needle clip one groove higher (reading was rich) or lower (reading was lean) to balance out the system. (See Fuel Systems.)

IMPORTANT: Make mixture changes gradually and carefully. Too lean a mixture, especially in two-strokes, can easily cause engine damage. In general, these engines should be set up to run as RICH as possible without fouling the plugs.

Between Tune-up Checks

Remove and inspect the spark plugs occasionally between tune-ups; any sudden changes will give you ample notice of an engine problem before it causes too much damage. For example, if one plug on a twin starts blistering, you know that the mixture must be lean, since the plug was normal at the last inspection. Therefore, you can immediately suspect some kind of air leak and check the possible sources before the lean mixture causes overheating and possibly piston seizure.

The point to remember is this: the more often you check plug condition, the less likely you are to receive a nasty surprise.

Cylinder Compression Check

Like spark plug readings, but more specific, regular compression checks will tell you when some part related to the combustion chamber is wearing out or has failed. It's a good idea to perform the following at least every other tune-up:

1. Remove the spark plug and screw a compression gauge into the hole (hold the automotive type firmly in the hole).

2. Hold the throttle grip WIDE OPEN and kick the engine over several times. Note the gauge indications.

In general, 50cc and 60cc two-stroke engines should read about 100 psi; 80cc to 125cc about 115-125 psi; 180cc to 200cc about 125-135 psi; large two-strokes 140-150 psi; and the XS1/XS2 four-stroke 130-145 psi.

Should the pressure suddenly drop after several good checks, you can suspect something serious—frozen rings, bad valves (XS1/XS2), etc. If the pressure drops gradually over a long period of time, normal wear is the cause and you can replace the worn out parts sometime before they cause an engine failure. If, on the other hand, pressure readings INCREASE, get out the blunt blade and start scraping off the carbon build-up.

By keeping track of combustion chamber pressure changes and making the necessary replacements or corrections, you can save the engine (and yourself) from larger and more expensive repair jobs.

Millimeters to Inches

MM	0	0.1	0.2	0.3	0.4	0.5	0.6	0.7	0.8	0.9
0	IN	.0039	.0079	.0118	.0157	.0197	.0236	.0276	.0315	.0354
1	.0394	.0433	.0472	.0512	.0551	.0591	.0630	.0669	.0709	.0748
2	.0787	.0827	.0866	.0906	.0945	.0984	.1024	.1063	.1102	.1142
3	.1181	.1200	.1260	.1299	.1339	.1378	.1417	.1457	.1496	.1535
4	.1575	.1614	.1654	.1693	.1732	.1772	.1811	.1850	.1890	.1929
5	.1969	.2000	.2047	.2087	.2126	.2165	.2205	.2244	.2283	.2323
6	.2362	.2402	.2441	.2480	.2520	.2559	.2598	.2638	.2677	.2717
7	.2756	.2795	.2835	.2874	.2913	.2953	.2992	.3031	.3071	.3110
8	.3150	.3189	.3228	.3268	.3307	.3346	.3386	.3425	.3465	.3504
9	.3543	.3583	.3622	.3661	.3701	.3740	.3780	.3819	.3858	.3898
10	.3937	.3976	.4016	.4055	.4094	.4134	.4173	.4213	.4252	.4291

.01 mm = .0004   .03 mm = .0012   .05 mm = .0020   .07 mm = .0028   .09 mm = .0035
.02 mm = .0008   .04 mm = .0016   .06 mm = .0024   .08 mm = .0031   .10 mm = .0039

Spark Plug Comparison Chart

Heat Range	NGK	Champion	AC	Auto-Lite	Bosch	KLG	Lodge	Reach	Thread Size
hot	B-4H	L14, L10	46FF, 45FF	AE52, AE6	W95T1, W145T1	F20, F50	B14, BN, CN		
	B-6HS	L90, L88, L86, L85	45F, M45FF, 44FF, M43FF	AE4, AE42	W175T1, W175T7	F70	CC14		
	B-7H	L7, L81	44F, 43F, 42F, 42FF	AE3, AE32, AE2, AE22	W200T7, W200T35, W225T1, W225T35	F75	HN, H14, HH14		
	B-7HZ	L5	M42FF, MC42F		W225T7	F80	2HN		
	B-7HC*							½″	14mm
	B-77HC*	L62R			W240T1, W240T16	F100	3HN		
	B-8H	L4J			W260T1				
	B-8HC*	L60R		AE903	W270T16				
	B-9H								
	B-9HC*	L57R		AE603	W310T16				
cold	B-10H	L54R							
hot	B-4E	N21, N18	47XL	AG9, AG7, AG52	W95T2, W125T2	FE20, FE30	BLN, BL14		
	B-6ES	N8, N84, N88, N6, N5	46N, 46XL, 45N, 45XL, C45XL, 44N, 44XL	AG5, AG4, AG42, AG3, AG32	W145T30, W160T2, W175T2, W175T30, W200T27, W200T30	FE50, FE70, FE75	CLNH, CC14, HBLN		
	B-7E, B-7ES		43N, 43XL	AG2, AG23	W225T2, W230T30	FE80	HLN	¾″	14mm
	B-7EC*	N4	C42N		W240T2, W240T28	FE100	2HLN		
	B-77EC*	N62R			W250P21, WG250T28	FE220			
	B-8E, B-8ES	N3	42XL		W260T28, W265P21	FE250	HLNP, 3HLN		
	B-9E	N60R							
cold	B-10E	N57R							

*Racing types with short electrode.

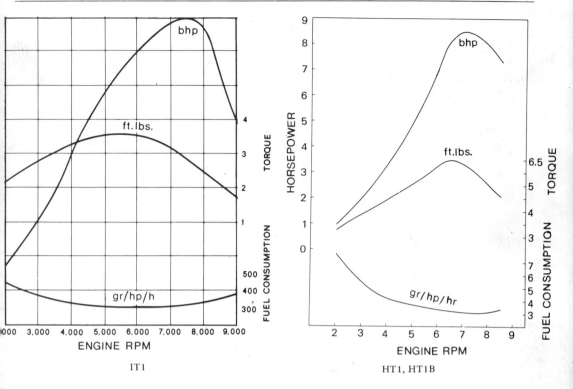

IT1

HT1, HT1B

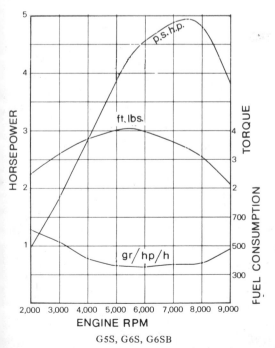

G5S, G6S, G6SB

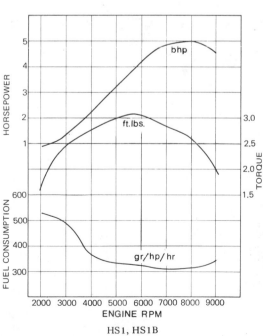

HS1, HS1B

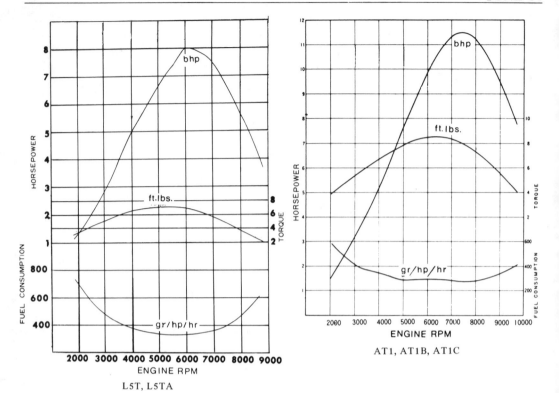

L5T, L5TA

AT1, AT1B, AT1C

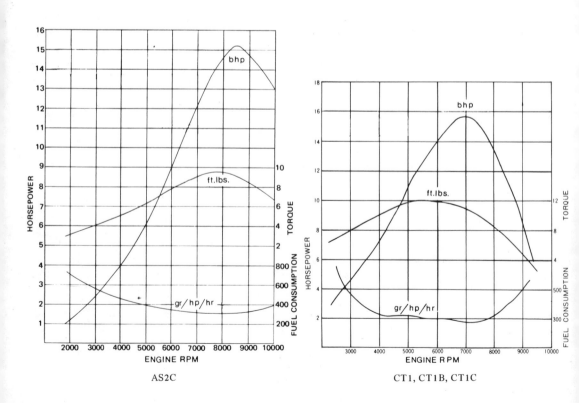

AS2C

CT1, CT1B, CT1C

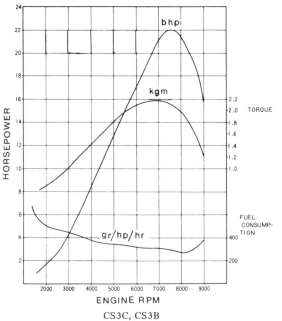

CS3C, CS3B

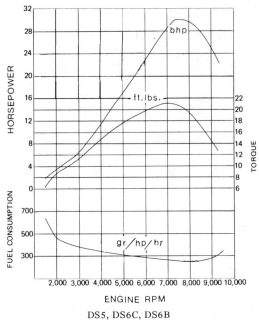

DS5, DS6C, DS6B

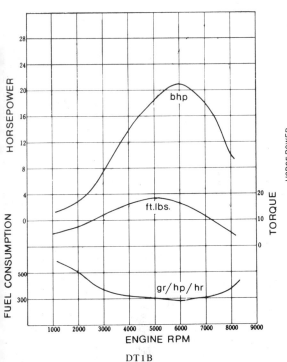

DT1B

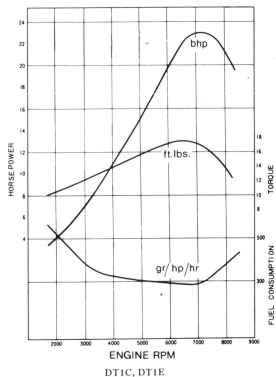

DT1C, DT1E

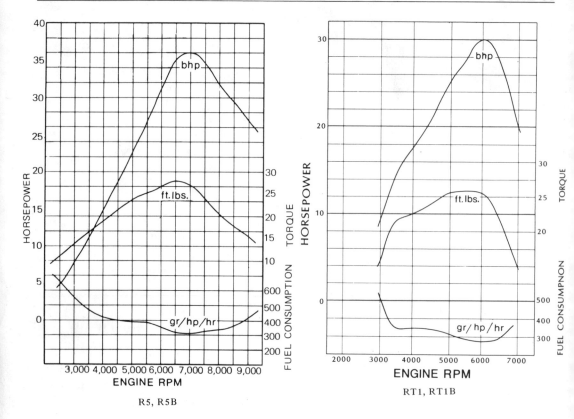

R5, R5B

RT1, RT1B

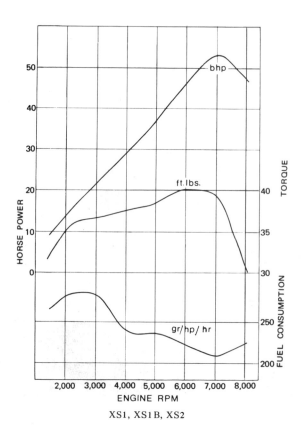

XS1, XS1B, XS2

Tune-Up Specifications

Model	Breaker Point Gap (mm)	Ignition Timing BTDC Adv.	Ret.	Spark Plug (NGK)	Spark Plug Gap (mm)	Spark Plug Tightening Torque (ft lbs)	Carburetor Air Screw (no. turns)	Idle Speed (rpm)	Throttle Cable Clearance 'A'/'B' (mm)	Oil Pump Adjustment Position	Minimum Oil Pump Stroke (mm)	Int Valve Clearance (mm/in)	Exht Valve Clearance (mm/in)
U5, U5L	0.20-0.40	1.7-1.9	—	B7HZ	0.6-0.7	18	1¼	1200-1400	0.0/1.5	Half Open	0.22-0.26	—	—
U5E	0.20-0.40	1.7-1.9	—	B7HZ	0.6-0.7	18	1¼	1200-1400	0.0/1.5	Half Open	0.22-0.26	—	—
U7E	0.30-0.40	1.7-1.9	—	B6HS	0.5-0.6	18	1¾	1200-1400	—	Idle	0.25-0.29	—	—
MJ2, MJ2T	0.30-0.35	2.1-2.3	—	B7HZ	0.6-0.7	18	¾	1200-1400	0.0/1.5	—	—	—	—
YJ1	0.20-0.40	2.0-2.2	—	B7HZ	0.6-0.7	18	1½	1200-1400	0.0/1.5	—	—	—	—
Early YJ2	0.20-0.40	1.7-1.9	—	B7HZ	0.6-0.7	18	1½	1200-1400	0.0/1.5	Half Open	0.22-0.26	—	—
Late YJ2	0.20-0.40	1.7-1.9	—	B8HC	0.6-0.7	18	1¾	1200-1400	0.0/1.5	Half Open	0.22-0.26	—	—
JT1	0.30-0.40	1.7-1.9	—	B7HS	0.5-0.6	18	1½	1200-1400	.75/1.5	Idle	0.20-0.25	—	—
JT2	0.30-0.40	1.7-1.9	—	B7HS	0.5-0.6	18	1¾	1200-1400	—	Half Open	0.30-0.35	—	—
MG1T	0.20-0.40	2.0-2.2	—	B7HZ	0.6-0.7	18	1½	1200-1400	0.0/1.5	—	—	—	—
YG1, YG1T	0.20-0.40	2.0-2.2	—	B7HZ	0.6-0.7	18	1½	1200-1400	0.0/1.5	—	—	—	—
YG1K, YG1KT	0.20-0.40	2.0-2.2	—	B7HZ	0.6-0.7	18	1¾	1200-1400	0.0/1.5	Half Open	0.22-0.26	—	—
YG5T	0.30-0.35	1.7-1.9	—	B7HZ	0.6-0.7	18	1½	1200-1400	0.0/1.5	Half Open	0.20-0.25	—	—
G5S	0.30-0.35	1.7-1.9	—	B7HZ	0.5-0.6	18	1¾	1200-1400	.75/1.5	Half Open	0.20-0.25	—	—
G6S	0.30-0.35	1.7-1.9	—	B7HZ	0.5-0.6	18	1¾	1200-1400	.75-1.5	Half Open	0.20-0.25	—	—
G6SB	0.30-0.40	1.7-1.9	—	B7HS	0.5-0.6	18	1¾	1200-1400	.75/1.5	Half Open	0.20-0.25	—	—
HT1	0.30-0.40	1.7-1.9	—	B8HC	0.5-0.6	18	1¾	1300-1500	.75/1.5	Idle	0.20-0.25	—	—
HT1B	0.30-0.40	1.7-1.9	—	B8ES	0.5-0.6	18	1¾	1300-1500	.75/1.5	Idle	0.20-0.25	—	—
HS1	0.30-0.35	1.7-1.9	—	B7HZ	0.5-0.6	18	1½	1100-1200	.75/0.0	Idle	0.20-0.25	—	—
HS1B	0.30-0.40	1.7-1.9	—	B9HC	0.5-0.6	18	1½	1100-1200	.75/0.0	Idle	0.20-0.25	—	—

① Given in mm except where indicated in degrees.
② May vary according to atmospheric conditions.
③ Cable 'A' at throttle grip; cable 'B' at carburetor top.

Tune-Up Specifications, continued

	Breaker Point Gap (mm)	Ignition① Timing BTDC Ret.	Ignition① Timing BTDC Adv.	Spark Plug (NGK)	Spark Plug Gap (mm)	Spark Plug Tightening Torque (ft lbs)	Carburetor② Air Screw (no. turns)	Idle Speed (rpm)	Throttle③ Cable Clearance 'A'/'B' (mm)	Oil Pump Adjustment Position	Minimum Oil Pump Stroke (mm)	Int Valve④ Clearance (mm/in)	Exht Valve④ Clearance (mm/in)
LS2	0.30-0.40	—	1.7-1.9	B7HS	0.5-0.6	18	1¾	1200-1400	—	Idle	0.20-0.25	—	—
YL2, YL2C	0.30-0.35	—	1.7-1.9	B7HZ	0.5-0.6	18	1½	1300-1500	0.0/1.5	Half Open	0.20-0.25	—	—
YL2CM	0.30-0.35	—	1.7-1.9	B8HC	0.5-0.6	18	1¾	1300-1500	0.0/1.5	Half Open	0.20-0.25	—	—
L5T, L5TA	0.30-0.35	—	1.7-1.9	B8HC	0.5-0.6	18	1¾	1300-1500	0.0/1.5	Half Open	0.20-0.25	—	—
LT2	0.30-0.40	—	1.7-1.9	B8HS	0.5-0.6	18	1¾	1100-1200	—	Idle	0.20-0.25	—	—
YL1, YL1E	0.30-0.35	—	1.7-1.9	B7HZ	0.5-0.6	18	2½	1200-1500	0.0/1.5	Idle	0.20-0.25	—	—
YA5	0.30-0.35	—	2.3-2.8	B7H	0.6-0.7	18	1¾	1300-1500	0.0/1.5	—	—	—	—
YA6	0.30-0.35	—	2.5-2.6	B7HZ	0.6-0.7	18	1¼	1300-1500	0.0/1.5	Half Open	0.22-0.26	—	—
AT1	0.30-0.35	—	1.7-1.9	B8E	0.5-0.6	18	1½	1400-1500	.75/1.5	Idle	0.20-0.25	—	—
AT1B	0.30-0.35	—	1.7-1.9	B8E	0.5-0.6	18	1½	1400-1500	.75/1.5	Idle	0.20-0.25	—	—
AT1C, AT2	0.30-0.40	—	1.7-1.9	B8ES	0.5-0.6	18	⑤	1400-1500	.75/1.5	Idle	0.20-0.25	—	—
YAS1(c)	0.30-0.35	—	1.7-1.9	B9HC	0.5-0.6	18	1¾	1200-1400	.75/0.0	Idle	0.20-0.25	—	—
AS2C	0.30-0.35	—	1.7-1.9	B9HC	0.5-0.6	18	1¾	1200-1400	.75/0.0	Idle	0.20-0.25	—	—
CT1	0.30-0.35	—	1.7-1.9	B8E	0.5-0.6	18	1½	1400-1500	.75/1.5	Idle	0.20-0.25	—	—
CT1B	0.30-0.35	—	1.7-1.9	B8E	0.5-0.6	18	1½	1400-1500	.75/1.5	Idle	0.20-0.25	—	—
CT1C, CT2	0.30-0.40	—	1.7-1.9	B8ES	0.5-0.6	18	⑥	1400-1500	.75/1.5	Idle	0.20-0.25	—	—
YCS1	0.30-0.35	—	1.7-1.9	B8HC	0.6-0.7	18	2	1100-1200	.75/0.0	Idle	0.20-0.25	—	—
YCS1C	0.30-0.35	—	1.7-1.9	B8HC	0.5-0.7	18	2¼	1100-1200	.75/0.0	Idle	0.20-0.25	—	—
CS3C	0.30-0.35	—	1.7-1.9	B9HC	0.5-0.6	18	2¼	1100-1200	.75/0.0	Idle	0.20-0.25	—	—
CS3B, CS5	0.30-0.40	—	1.7-1.9	⑦	0.5-0.6	18	2	1100-1200	.75/0.0	Idle	0.20-0.25	—	—
DT1	0.30-0.35	—	3.1-3.3	B7E	0.5-0.6	18	1½	1400-1500	.75/0.0	Idle	0.20-0.25	—	—
DT1S	0.30-0.35	—	3.1-3.3	B7E(N)	0.5-0.6	18	1½	1400-1500	.75/0.0	Idle	0.20-0.25	—	—

DT1B	0.30–0.35	—	3.1–3.3	B7E(N)	0.5–0.6	18	$1\frac{1}{2}$	1400–1500	.75/0.0	Idle	0.20–0.25	—	—
DT1C	0.30–0.35	—	3.1–3.3	B7E	0.5–0.6	18	$1\frac{1}{2}$	1400–1500	.75/0.0	Idle	0.20–0.25	—	—
DT1E, DT2	0.30–0.40	—	3.1–3.3	B8ES	0.5–0.6	18	$1\frac{1}{2}$	1400–1500	.75/0.0	Idle	0.20–0.25	—	—
YD3	0.30–0.35	—	2.1–2.3	B7HZ	0.6–0.7	18	$1\frac{1}{4}$	1100–1200	0.0/1.5	—	—	—	—
YDT1	0.30–0.35	—	2.1–2.3	B7HZ	0.6–0.7	18	$1\frac{1}{4}$	1100–1200	0.0/1.5	—	—	—	—
YDS1	0.30–0.35	—	2.5–3.0	B6H	0.6–0.7	18	$1\frac{1}{2}$	1100–1200	0.0/1.5	—	—	—	—
YDS2	0.30–0.35	—	1.7–1.8	B7HZ	0.6–0.7	18	$1\frac{1}{2}$	1100–1200	0.0/1.5	—	—	—	—
YDS3	0.30–0.35	—	1.8–1.9	B77HC	0.6–0.7	18	$1\frac{1}{2}$	1100–1200	.75/1.5	Idle	0.22–0.26	—	—
YDS3C	0.30–0.35	—	1.7–1.9	B8HC	0.6–0.7	18	$1\frac{1}{2}$	1100–1200	.75/1.5	Idle	0.22–0.26	—	—
YDS5	0.30–0.35	—	1.7–1.9	B8HC	0.6–0.7	18	$1\frac{1}{2}$	1000–1200	.75/0.0	Idle	0.20–0.25	—	—
DS6/DS6C	0.30–0.35	—	1.7–1.9	B7HZ	0.5–0.6	18	$1\frac{1}{2}$	1100–1200	.75/0.0	Idle	0.20–0.25	—	—
DS6B	0.30–0.35	—	1.7–1.9	B9HC	0.5–0.6	18	$1\frac{1}{2}$	1100–1200	.75/0.0	Idle	0.20–0.25	—	—
DS7	0.30–0.40	—	1.9–2.1	B8HS	0.5–0.6	18	$1\frac{1}{2}$	1100–1200	—	Idle	0.20–0.25	—	—
YM1	0.30–0.35	—	1.9–2.0	B8HC	0.6–0.7	18	$1\frac{1}{2}$	1100–1200	.75/0.0	Idle	0.20–0.25	—	—
YM2C	0.30–0.35	—	2.0–2.2	B8HC	0.6–0.7	18	$1\frac{1}{2}$	1000–1200	.75/0.0	Idle	0.20–0.25	—	—
YR1	0.30–0.35	—	2.0–2.2	B8HC	0.6–0.7	18	$2\frac{1}{4}$	1000–1200	.75/0.0	Idle	0.20–0.25	—	—
YR2, YR2C	0.30–0.35	—	2.0–2.2	B9HC	0.5–0.6	18	$1\frac{1}{2}$	1200–1400	.75/0.0	Idle	0.20–0.25	—	—
R3C	0.30–0.35	—	2.0–2.2	B9HC	0.5–0.6	18	$1\frac{1}{2}$	1200–1400	.75/0.0	Idle	0.20–0.25	—	—
R5/R5B	0.30–0.40	—	1.9–2.1	B9HC	0.5–0.6	18	$1\frac{3}{4}$	1300–1400	.75/0.0	Idle	0.20–0.25	—	—
RT1	0.30–0.35	—	3.3–3.5	B7E	0.5–0.6	18	$1\frac{1}{4}$	1400–1500	.75/0.0	Idle	0.20–0.25	—	—
RT1B	0.30–0.40	—	2.8–3.0	B9ES	0.5–0.6	18	$1\frac{3}{4}$	1400–1500	.75/0.0	Idle	0.20–0.25	—	—
XS1	0.30–0.35	13–17°	40°	B8E	0.5–0.6	18	$\frac{1}{2}$	1000–1200	1.0/—	—	—	.15/.006	.30/.012
XS1B	0.30–0.35	13–17°	40°	B8E	0.5–0.6	18	1	1000–1200	1.0/—	—	—	.15/.006	.30/.012
XS2	0.30–0.40	13–17°	42°	B8ES	0.5–0.6	18	$\frac{3}{4}$	1000–1200	—	—	—	.15/.006	.30/.012

① Given in mm except where indicated in degrees.
② May vary according to atmospheric conditions.
③ Cable 'A' at throttle grip; cable 'B' at carburetor top.
④ Cold.
⑤ AT1—$1\frac{1}{2}$; AT2—$1\frac{3}{4}$
⑥ CT1—$1\frac{1}{2}$; CT2—2
⑦ CS3—B9HC; CS5—B9HS
⑧ R5/R5B—B9HC; R5C—B9HS
⑨ R5/R5B—$1\frac{3}{4}$; R5C—$1\frac{1}{4}$
⑩ RT1—$1\frac{3}{4}$; RT2—$1\frac{1}{2}$

4 ● Engine and Transmission

Two-Stroke Models

Engine Operation

With the exception of the 653cc XS1/XS2, all Yamahas use either piston-port or rotary-valve two-stroke engines. The following discussion of each type will provide some insight into how they work and may someday prove very helpful in troubleshooting.

Piston Port Two-Stroke

The piston port two-stroke is the simplest of all engines commonly seen in motorcycle application. It has only three main moving parts and uses ports, rather than valves, (as in four-stroke engines) to regulate intake and exhaust flow. These ports are all located in the cylinder wall and are opened and closed by the piston's movement. Their functions are:

Intake Port—admits fresh fuel mixture from the carburetor into the crankcase.

Transfer Ports—provide passages for the fuel mixture between the crankcase and combustion chamber. (Also known as scavenging ports.)

Exhaust Port—releases burnt gases from the combustion chamber into the exhaust pipe.

Basically, this is what happens during a 360° rotation of the crankshaft, beginning with the piston at top dead center:

1. DOWNSTROKE

The piston descends from the previous cycle and exposes the exhaust port, letting out the expanding burnt gases. Simultaneously, the piston's downward movement compresses the fuel mixture from the previous cycle occupying the airtight crankcase.

As the piston continues to descend, it also exposes the transfer ports; the compressed mixture waiting in the crankcase now rushes through the ports and fills the combustion chamber, while at the same time sweeping any remaining burnt gases out the exhaust port.

2. UPSTROKE

After reaching its lowest point of travel, the piston begins to ascend and closes off the transfer ports. At the same time, the piston's upward movement creates a partial vacuum in the crankcase.

As the piston continues to ascend, it closes off the exhaust port and begins to compress the mixture in the combustion chamber. Meanwhile, the bottom of the piston exposes the intake port and a fresh fuel mixture is sucked into the crankcase. When the piston approaches top dead center, ignition occurs and the piston once again descends to begin another cycle.

As described, ignition occurs once every 360° or, more appropriately, once every two strokes of the piston (one down and one up). Hence, the term two-stroke engine.

A recent improvement in piston port design is the five-port cylinder, and the main difference between it and the conventional-type

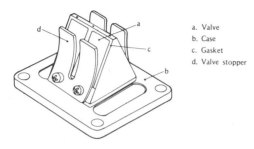

a. Valve
b. Case
c. Gasket
d. Valve stopper

Conventional three-port exhaust sweep

lies in the five-part cylinder's more efficient exhaust sweep. The earlier Schnuerle loop scavenging system has two transfer ports that aim streams of fresh mixture toward the back of the cylinder; this sweeps out most of the remaining exhaust gases, but leaves one area untouched in the middle of the combustion chamber. The five-port system, on the other hand, has two additional auxilary transfer ports. These extra ports direct a small charge of fresh mixture right at the dead spot and force it out the exhaust port. This complete exhaust sweep creates more space for the incoming mixture and, as a result, the engine has more low- and mid-range power, runs cooler, and consumes less fuel.

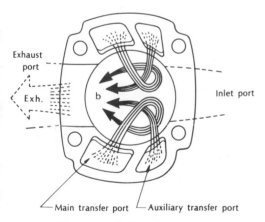

Exhaust port

Exh.

Inlet port

b

Main transfer port — Auxiliary transfer port

Five-port cylinder exhaust sweep

Another recent innovation is the employment of teflon-coated keystone-type rings on both piston port and rotary-valve engines. Whereas the conventional ring has a rectangular cross-section and piston groove, the keystone ring has a beveled top edge. The piston groove is tapered to match it (see illustration). Essentially, its advantages are:

1. During the fuel mixture's combustion, the pressure forces the ring tighter against the cylinder wall, thereby forming a better seal, and

2. The ring's back and forth movement (as pressure is applied and relieved) creates a scrubbing action which prevents the build-up of gum deposits.

The newest development from Yamaha engineering is the seven-port cylinder used in conjunction with a reed valve. The valve consists of a die-cast aluminum block with flexible stainless steel reeds that serve to open and close the intake port. The reeds are actuated by crankcase vacuum and, therefore, admit only the necessary amount of fuel. When combined with the improved scavenging ability of the seven-port cylinder, the valve helps reduce fuel consumption, increase low-end pull and flatten out the horsepower and torque curves.

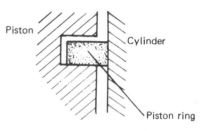

Piston

Cylinder

Piston ring

Conventional ring and piston groove cross section

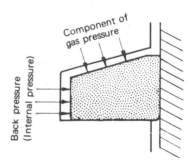

Component of gas pressure

Back pressure (Internal pressure)

This is how combustion pressure forces the keystone ring against the cylinder wall for a better seal

Rotary-Valve Two-Stroke

The rotary-valve two-stroke engine operates by the same basic principles as the piston port type, but is constructed differently and offers some distinct advantages.

The valve itself is a resin-hardened fiber disc with a cutaway section along its circumference. The disc is mounted directly to the end of the crankshaft and enclosed within a narrow sealed chamber; on one side is the crankcase intake port and on the other side is the carburetor. As the engine rotates, the cutaway section of the valve exposes the port and allows fresh fuel mixture to be sucked into the crankcase; when the cutaway section ends, the port is sealed by the disc and no more mixture can enter.

What is the advantage? In the piston port two-stroke, the intake port is located in the cylinder wall along the transfer and exhaust ports; therefore, intake timing (WHEN the port opens and closes) is dictated by the piston skirt and limited by the size and position of the other ports. In the rotary-valve type, on the other hand, the intake port is located in the side of the crankcase, and intake timing is determined by the position (on the disc) and duration of the valve cutaway.

This independence from piston control and cylinder design complications allows intake timing to be set (and easily adjusted) for optimum engine breathing. As a result, the engine has greater flexibility and delivers more power throughout a wider range.

Although the rotary-valve system is far more efficient, it is currently used only on a few Yamaha single-cylinder engines. The reasons for this are:

1. The engine cases would have to be widened excessively in order to accommodate the system in a twin or any of today's very narrow dirt bikes.

2. The recent development of the five-port cylinder has sufficiently increased the piston port type's power output so that, in most cases, the rotary-valve is an unnecessary complication.

Transmission Description

Yamaha two-stroke engines are mated to a three-, four-, five-, or six-speed (three-speed, two-range) constant-mesh transmission via primary gears (except the YA5, which uses a chain) and a wet multi-disc type manual or centrifugal clutch. Although they vary from model to model and year to year, they all share the same basic construction. The most notable differences and improvements are in the gear change mechanisms which employ either a rotating drum or a cam-plate type shifter.

Since Yamaha transmissions are similar and their operation is conventional, detailed descriptions will not be given.

Engine Removal

The following procedures apply to the machines given in the appropriate headings. Some steps vary from model to model, but as many

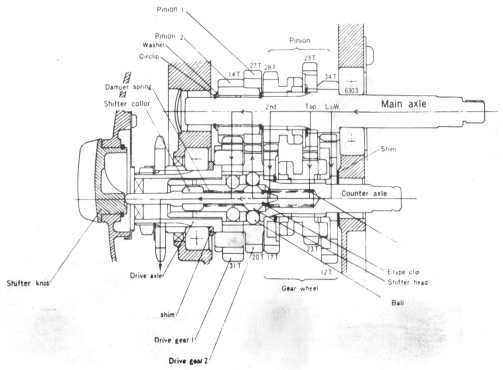

L5T three-speed, two-range transmission layout

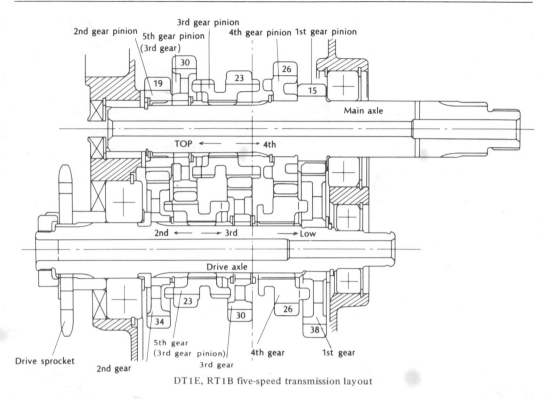

2nd gear pinion 5th gear pinion (3rd gear) 3rd gear pinion 4th gear pinion 1st gear pinion

30 19 23 26 15

Main axle

TOP ← → 4th

2nd ← → 3rd → Low

Drive axle

23 34 30 26 38

Drive sprocket 2nd gear 5th gear (3rd gear pinion) 3rd gear 4th gear 1st gear

DT1E, RT1B five-speed transmission layout

of these differences as possible have been noted.

Use the proper metric tools for all work and be sure to lay out and mark all parts as they are being removed. Special tools are required in several steps, so refer to the end of this chapter to see what is needed. Some of these tools can be substituted but others cannot.

Also, it's a good idea to clean thoroughly the entire bike (especially around the engine) before beginning any repairs: this will prevent dirt from entering and will make it easier for you to see and remove attaching nuts and bolts.

Removing the exhaust pipe ring nut

All Models With Rotary-Valve Engines Except YG5T, L5T and the JT1/JT2 Mini Enduro

1. Warm up the engine for a few minutes, then drain the gearbox oil. Reinstall the drain plug(s).

2. Remove the exhaust pipe ring nut, using the special wrench. Be careful not to damage the cylinder!

3. If the exhaust pipe and muffler are connected by a flange ring nut, loosen the nut and swing the exhaust pipe out of the way. If the exhaust pipe and muffler are one unit, remove all muffler mounting bolts and lift off the entire assembly.

Removing the exhaust pipe and muffler as an assembly

4. Remove the gearshift pedal.

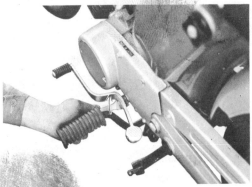

Removing the gearshift pedal

5. Remove the left crankcase cover.
6. If equipped with a magneto:
  a. Disconnect the wiring harness at its center connector (behind side cover or under seat).
  b. Remove the magneto flywheel, using the special puller tool.

Removing the flywheel magneto

  c. Remove the phillips-head mounting screws and the magneto base plate.

Removing the magneto base plate

  d. Tie the magneto base plate to the frame, somewhere out of the way.

Keep the magneto base plate out of the way for the remaining steps of engine removal

7. If equipped with a generator:
  a. Disconnect the wiring harness terminals at the generator.

Disconnecting the DC generator wiring harness

NOTE: On some early models, the wiring harness must be disconnected in the battery compartment because the generator terminals are soldered.

  b. On models equipped with a governor, remove the mounting bolt and the governor assembly.
  c. Remove the attaching screws and the generator yoke assembly.
  d. Remove the armature bolt and breaker can.

Removing the DC generator armature bolt and breaker cam

e. Remove the generator armature, using the special puller bolt.

8. Pry out the crankshaft Woodruff key, using a narrow straight-slot screwdriver.

Removing the crankshaft Woodruff key

9. If the machine is equipped with a fully enclosed chain, remove the lower half of the cover.

10. Disconnect the master link and remove the drive chain. This is a good time to give the chain a solvent soak.

Disconnecting the final drive chain master link

11. Remove the carburetor/oil pump cover.

Removing the carburetor/oil pump cover

12. Make sure the fuel petcock is shut off, then disconnect and plug the fuel line at the carburetor.

13. Remove the attaching screw at the front of the crankcase, then lift out the carburetor. To separate the throttle cable from the carburetor, remove the knurled cap and pull out the throttle slide.

NOTE: If no carburetor repairs are needed, leave the fuel line and throttle cable connected, and tie the assembly out of the way.

Removing the carburetor securing screw

14. Disconnect the oil supply line at the Autolube tank and cover the fitting with a short piece of plugged hose.

An extra piece of oil line tied in a knot will serve to plug the Autolube tank

15. Turn the oil pump pulley against its spring and disconnect the cable, then remove the adjusting bracket screws and tie the cable and bracket out of the way.

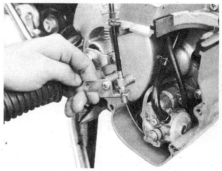

Disconnect the oil pump cable and adjuster bracket as an assembly

16. On models with a manual clutch, remove the clutch adjusting screw, if necessary, then the clutch arm and spring. Disconnect the cable from the arm and spring, then unscrew the cable adjustment nut on the crankcase cover and pull the cable end through. Tie it out of the way.

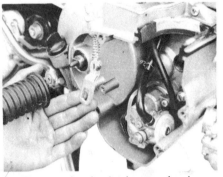

Disconnecting the clutch arm and spring

17. Remove the air cleaner element and housing, if necessary, or disconnect the rubber elbow at the housing or case cover.

18. Disconnect the spark plug lead.

19. Remove the two upper engine mounting bolts and loosen the footrest mounting bolt.

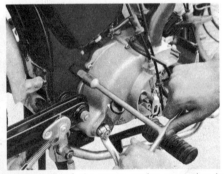

Removing one of the upper engine mounting bolts

20. Hold the engine tilted slightly downward and disconnect the neutral switch wire. This is a good time to make certain nothing remains connected or is hanging in the way.

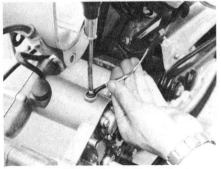

Disconnecting the neutral switch wire

21. Support the bottom of the engine and remove the footrest mounting bolt. Lift the unit out of the frame.

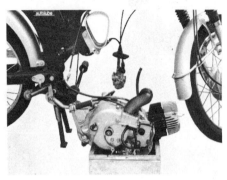

Now that the engine is removed and intact, put it on a bench before you trip over it

YG5T AND L5T MODELS

This removal procedure is basically the same as the preceding, but first the downtube support and engine protector (bash plate) must be removed.

JT1/JT2 MINI ENDURO

The JT1 engine is mounted in a double-loop cradle frame (same as full sized Enduros). The removal procedure is basically the same as for the other rotary-valve singles, with the exception of the following points:

1. Before removing the muffler assembly, the seat mounting pin must be removed and the seat pulled back and off.

Removing the JT1 seat

2. Also remove the gas tank front mounting bolt and lift off the tank. Remember to plug the fuel line.

3. Disconnect the magneto wiring underneath the gas tank.

4. Disconnect the neutral switch wiring before removing the engine mounting bolts.

JT1 gas tank front mounting bolt

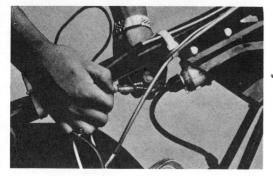

Disconnecting the JT1 magneto wiring

FULL SIZE ENDURO MODELS

1. Warm up the engine, then drain the gearbox oil and reinstall the drain plug(s).

2. Remove the attaching ring nut, bolts, retaining springs, and the muffler/exhaust pipe assembly.

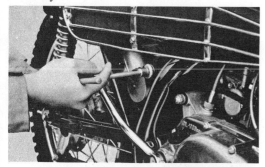

Muffler mounting bolt

Enduro muffler assembly mounting bolt

3. Remove the gearshift pedal.

4. Remove the lefthand case cover(s). Disconnect the clutch cable and tie it aside.

5. Disconnect the master link and remove the chain.

6. If equipped with a generator, disconnect the wiring harness terminals at the generator stator. If equipped with a magneto, disconnect the wiring harness at its center connector.

7. Remove the generator yoke assembly and armature, or the magneto flywheel as described in rotary-valve engine removal.

8. Disconnect the neutral switch wire.

9. Disconnect the spark plug lead and tie it out of the way.

NOTE: On the RT1B, also disconnect the compression release cable.

10. Remove the oil pump cover on the other side of the engine. Turn the pump pulley against its spring, then slip off the cable end.

11. Disconnect the oil pump supply line at the Autolube tank and cover the fitting with a short piece of plugged hose.

12. Disconnect the tachometer drive cable.

Disconnecting the tachometer drive cable

13. Disconnect and plug the fuel line at the carburetor.

14. Remove the air cleaner rubber elbow.

Removing the air cleaner elbow

NOTE: On the HT1, remove the air cleaner assembly.

15. Twist off the knurled carburetor cap after pulling back the rubber dust cover.

16. Pull out the carburetor throttle slide, then tie it and the throttle cable to the frame.

17. Remove the attaching nuts or clamp screws and the carburetor.

Removing the carburetor

18. Remove the engine mounting bolts and lift out the powerplant.

Removing the engine front mounting bolt

Twin Cylinder Engines

1. Warm up the engine and drain the gearbox oil, then reinstall the drain plug(s).

2. Remove the toolbox side cover.

3. Remove the exhaust pipe ring nut or stud nuts. If the exhaust pipe and muffler are connected by a flange ring nut, unscrew the nut and swing the exhaust pipes out of the way; if they cannot be separated, remove all attaching bolts and the entire exhaust assembly.

4. Remove the left footrest and the gearshift pedal.

NOTE: On some models, both right and left footrests must be removed as an assembly; on others (such as the R5), there is sufficient clearance without removing either footrest.

5. Remove all case covers.

6. Disconnect the clutch cable and tie it aside.

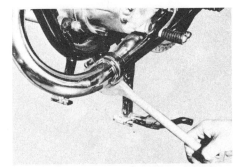

Unscrewing the exhaust pipe/muffler flange ring nut

On the R5, the clutch cable can remain attached to the case cover

7. Disconnect the wiring harness at the generator terminals or the alternator center connector, and at the neutral switch.

Disconnecting the alternator wiring harness

8. Remove the yoke mounting screws and the yoke assembly.

Removing the yoke assembly

9. Remove the armature bolt, governor, and breaker cam.

10. Remove the generator or alternator armature, using the special puller bolt.

Removing the alternator armature

11. Remove the crankshaft Woodruff key with a harrow slot-head screwdriver.

12. Disconnect the tachometer drive cable.

13. Disconnect the master link and remove the chain.

14. Turn the oil pump pulley against its spring, then slip out the end of the cable.

15. Unscrew the oil pump cable adjuster and pull the cable through the hole.

NOTE: Some models have the oil pump cable situated between the crankcase and the case cover. On these machines, simply pull out the rubber grommet and remove the adjuster bracket screws. Then tie the cable and bracket assembly out of the way.

16. Disconnect and plug the fuel lines at the carburetors.

17. Remove the attaching clamp screws and disconnect the air cleaner rubber elbows from the carburetors.

NOTE: Remove the air cleaner assemblies on the HS1, YAS1, AS2 and early YDS models.

18. Pull back the rubber dust covers and unscrew the knurled carburetor caps. Pull out the throttle slide assemblies and tie them out of the way (leave the cables attached).

Carburetor throttle slide removed

19. Remove the attaching clamps or bolts and disconnect the starter jet linkage, then remove the carburetors. This is not really necessary, but if the engine is being torn down beyond the cylinder head, they will have to come off sooner or later.

20. Disconnect the spark plug leads.

21. On 250, 305, and 350cc models, remove the engine in the following manner:

a. Remove the four engine mounting bolts.
NOTE: On the R5, also remove the upper rear mounting plate.

b. Straddle the bike and hold the engine by the cylinder cooling fins on one side and by the kickstarter on the other.

c. Pull the engine back slightly, then lift it out the left side of the frame.

22. On the 90, 125, 180, and 200cc models:

a. Support the bottom of the engine on a box or have a helper hold it up.

b. Remove all mounting bolts, then lift the engine up and out the left side of the frame.

23. On the 100cc YL1 models:

a. Loosen all engine mounting bolts.

b. Remove all but the lower downtube and the lower rear mounting bolts.

c. Hold up the front of the engine and remove the downtube mounting bolt, then swing the front support out of the way.

d. Let the engine tilt downward onto a box, then remove the lower rear mounting bolt.

Engine Installation

All Models

Installation is basically a reversal of the removal procedures, but the following points should be noted:

1. Apply a small amount of grease to the crankshaft before installing the magneto flywheel, alternator or generator armature; this will prevent them from freezing on the shaft.

2. When installing the carburetors, make certain that the manifold flange and carburetor slots (if so equipped) do NOT align.

3. Replace any worn exhaust pipe and muffler ring nut gaskets.

4. Make certain that the fuel and oil line circlips are properly seated.

5. Make certain that the engine mounting bolts are tightened down securely. If possible, use a torque wrench (see Torque Specifications at the end of this chapter).

6. After bleeding the oil pump and refilling the gearbox, check all points of adjustment—cables, chain, rear brake, ignition timing, carburetor synchronization, oil pump plunger stroke, etc.

Engine Disassembly and Repair

The following procedures are generalized when they apply to all two-stroke models and given under separate headings when they differ. When applicable on twins you can interpret "cylinder," or "piston," etc., to mean BOTH cylinders, pistons, etc.

Cleanliness and careful approach are IMPERATIVE! A quick ring job could become a complete engine disassembly if simple precautions are not taken. Lay out and mark the parts in sequence as they are being removed: this way the correct order of reassembly will be obvious. If possible, clean all the engine parts in solvent and blow them dry with compressed air. When cleaning ball or roller bearings, don't spin them until they have been thoroughly cleaned and dried: particles in the solvent bath often get caught in the bearing races and only high pressure air will remove them.

A good general rule to follow when disassembling an unfamiliar engine is to restrain yourself. When a nut or bolt seems to require an inordinate amount of pressure to loosen it, don't just give it the old "heave-ho" effort. Instead: sit back, relax for a few minutes, and then survey the situation. More engine damage is caused by swinging a heavy wrench than most other causes combined, and the reason is usually a securing bolt unseen by a mechanic who is blinded with frustration. These engines contain a lot of aluminum alloy and you have to be careful!

Many operations can be performed with the engine mounted in the frame. However, any repairs requiring splitting the crankcase halves must be done on a bench.

Cylinder Head

All Models

The cylinder head is made of an aluminum alloy (for heat dissipation qualities) and is attached to the cylinder with four nuts and washers. Remove the spark plug and back off the nuts slowly in an X pattern, then lift off the

head and gasket. Remove the carbon build-up with a blunt blade as described in Maintenance. Inspect the head for any cracks or signs of damage.

When installing the cylinder head, replace the gasket if it is old or damaged. Tighten the nuts up to torque specifications a little at a time in an X pattern.

Loosen the head nuts a little at a time in an X pattern

Cylinder head gasket

Cylinder

All Models
REMOVAL

Disconnect the oil line banjo fitting at the base of the cylinder, then tap the bottom cooling fins with a rubber mallet. Separate the cylinder from the crankcase and, as soon as there is enough room, stuff some CLEAN rags into the case opening. Lift off the cylinder and base gasket, being careful to hold the piston when it falls free of the cylinder.

INSPECTION

Scrape carbon accumulation out of the exhaust and transfer port area with a blunt blade. Also remove the carbon ridge at the top of the

Arrow indicates the oil line banjo fitting

Tap LIGHTLY with a rubber mallet to remove the cylinder

cylinder. If necessary, use #400 sandpaper in a crosshatch pattern.

Look closely for any cracks or seizure spots, then measure the cylinder with an inside-diameter micrometer or cylinder gauge.

Most wear occurs at the upper part of the cylinder due to piston side thrust and heat expansion characteristics. Therefore, the cylinder won't be perfectly cylindrical. Make eight measurements at the points indicated in the illustration, and, if the difference between the minimum and maximum diameters exceeds 0.05 mm (0.0019 in.), the cylinder should be rebored and honed.

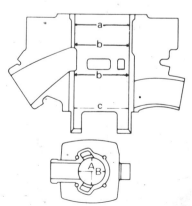

Cylinder diameter measuring points

Using a dial gauge to measure bore diameter

BORING AND HONING

The cylinder should be bored and then honed in a crosshatch pattern so that its minimum inside diameter will be equal to the replacement piston's maximum diameter PLUS the minimum piston-to-cylinder wall clearance (see Specifications).

NOTE: Replacement pistons are available in 0.25 mm (0.010 in.) and 0.50 mm (0.020 in.) oversizes for all models, and several additional sizes up to 1.00 mm (0.040 in.) can be obtained for the YDS series. These sizes vary slightly from piston to piston, however, so if you want to do a real careful job, get the replacement piston FIRST, then bore and hone the cylinder to match it.

After boring and honing, recheck the diameter measurements and make certain that the difference between minimum and maximum cylinder diameters does not exceed 0.01 mm (0.0004 in.). And finally, chamfer the intake, exhaust, and transfer ports so that there are no rough edges.

INSTALLATION

Install a new base gasket, then slide the cylinder down over the studs to a point above the piston. Position the end gaps of the piston rings at their respective knock (locating) pins and squeeze them into their grooves with a ring compressor or, if necessary, your fingers. Insert the top of the piston, then CAREFULLY slide the cylinder down over the rings and piston skirt. Remove the rags and slide the cylinder down to the crankcase, then reconnect the oil line banjo fitting.

Install new cylinder base gaskets carefully

Removing the piston pin circlips

NOTE: An automotive radiator hose clamp makes a very inexpensive and efficient ring compressor. Select a clamp approximately the same size as the piston and slip it around the rings. Tighten the clamp enough to compress and hold the rings, in their grooves, but loose enough to be pushed off. When the cylinder is lowered over the rings, it will push the clamp down around the piston skirt where you can then loosen and remove it.

Squeezing the rings together with your fingers will usually suffice when working on single-cylinder engines

Piston

All Models

REMOVAL AND DISASSEMBLY

Once again, make sure that the crankcase opening is covered by some clean rags, then, if the factory stamp is obscured, mark the piston crown for reassembly. Remove the piston pin circlips with a pair of needle-nose pliers and push the pin out through the piston with your finger or a straight-slot screwdriver.

NOTE: It may be necessary to heat the piston slightly to remove the pin. Soak a rag in boiling water, wring it out and apply it to the piston; if that fails, use a torch set on a very low flame.

Place the piston away from the engine, then CAREFULLY spread the top piston ring apart with your thumbs and slide it off the piston. Remove the other ring in the same manner.

Removing the piston rings

INSPECTION

PISTON PIN—push the pin into the piston bore: the fit should be snug, but loose enough to move with your fingers (with some effort). If the fit is too loose, replace the pin and/or the piston.

Checking piston pin fit

Check the center of the pin for step wear by inserting it into the connecting rod small-end bearing. If there is any up-and-down freeplay, replace the pin AND the bearing.

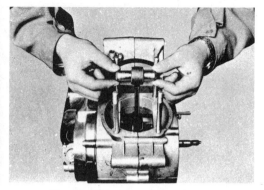

Checking the piston pin for step wear

PISTON RINGS—Remove any carbon accumulation and note their general condition, then push one of the rings into the cylinder with the piston, keeping it parallel to the bottom of the bore.

Using a white piece of paper as a reflector, make a visual check for any spaces between the ring and the cylinder wall, then measure the ring end gap with a feeler gauge. If there are any spaces between the ring and cylinder, or the end gap is not within specifications, replace the ring. Check the other ring in the same manner.

Measuring ring end gap

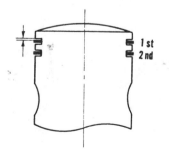

No. 1 ring 0.0016-0.0031 in. (0.04-0.08 mm)
No. 2 ring 0.0012-0.0028 in. (0.03-0.07 mm)

Ring land clearance

On earlier models not equipped with keystone rings, also measure the clearance between the rings and ring lands (see illustration).

PISTON—Remove carbon deposits from the piston crown with a blunt blade and clean out the ring grooves with a narrow piece of metal.

NOTE: Do not use a broken ring to clean the grooves of a piston with the letter K stamped after the size number (located on the piston crown). These pistons are the keystone-type; an old ring will not fit into the groove and may cause damage if forced.

Inspect the piston for any hairline cracks or wear spots on the skirt. These spots usually indicate that the piston has seized to one degree or another (not necessarily frozen). To prevent the spot from causing a future seizure, lightly sand the area with #400 sandpaper.

Sanding piston seizure spots

When cold, the piston has a slightly oval shape and is tapered at the top. This is to compensate for heat expansion so that the piston will assume a cylindrical shape when it reaches normal operating temperatures. Measure the piston with a micrometer at right angles to the pin bosses and 10 mm (approximately 7/16 in.) from the bottom of the skirt, then use this figure in conjunction with cylinder diameter measurements to determine if cylinder reboring is necessary. If it is, an oversize replacement piston will also be required.

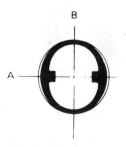

Measure piston diameter at 'A' and 'B'

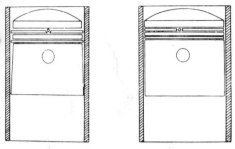

Piston shape cold at left, warm at right

Using a micrometer to measure piston diameter

ASSEMBLY AND INSTALLATION

Hold the bottom piston ring with the markings facing up and spread it apart slightly, then slide it over the top of the piston and into its groove. Do the same with the top ring, then align both ring end gaps with their respective knock (locating) pins.

NOTE: Keystone rings are marked #1 (top) and #2 (bottom). They are NOT interchangeable with the conventional-type rings, nor are keystone pistons interchangable with conventional pistons.

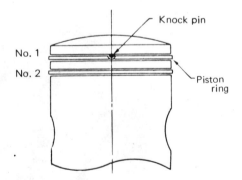

Piston ring knock pin location

Position the piston over the connecting rod with the arrow (stamped on the crown) facing toward the front of the engine, then push the piston pin through the piston and connecting

rod bearing. Make sure the crankcase opening is covered, then install the piston pin circlips.

Piston installation

Right Crankcase Cover

All Models

1. Remove the kickstarter lever.

Removing the kickstart lever

2. On rotary valve engines, disconnect the oil line banjo bolt at the delivery pipe.

3. Remove the attaching screws and lift off the case cover with oil pump in place.

NOTE: It may be necessary to tap the cover with a rubber mallet to aid removal.

4. Remove the case cover gasket.

Removing the right case cover

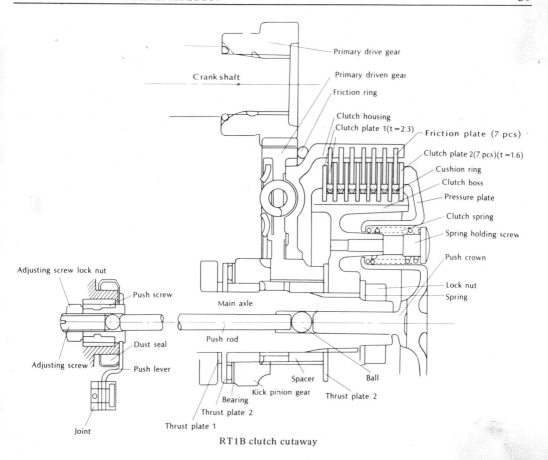

RT1B clutch cutaway

INSTALLATION

Installation is a reversal of the removal procedure with the addition of the following:

1. Apply Yamaha bond #5 to mating case and case-cover surfaces.
2. Replace the case-cover gasket.

Removing the clutch spring retaining screws

Clutch

Manual

REMOVAL AND DISASSEMBLY

1. Remove the clutch spring retaining screws and pressure plate.
2. Pull out the clutch springs and pushrod.
3. Hold the clutch boss with the special holding tool, bend back the lockwasher tab, and remove the boss locknut.

Removing the clutch pushrod

4. Remove the clutch boss, cushion rings, and friction plates.

Removing the clutch boss locknut

INSPECTION

CLUTCH SPRINGS—Measure the free length of the clutch springs. If 1.0 mm (or more) shorter than specified, replace the spring(s).

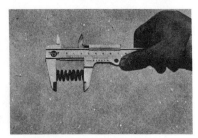

Measuring clutch spring free length

FRICTION PLATES—Measure the thickness of the friction plates. If 0.3 mm (or more) thinner than specified, replace the plate(s).

Measuring friction plate thickness

PUSHROD—Roll the pushrod on a flat surface to make sure it isn't bent.

SPACER—Check the inside and outside spacer surfaces for any nicks, scratches or burrs. Smooth out any rough surfaces with #400 sandpaper, then install the spacer in the primary driven gear. If there is more than

0.048 mm clearance between the spacer and driven gear, replace the spacer and/or driven gear.

Checking spacer clearance in the primary driven gear (clutch housing)

Install the spacer on the transmission shaft and measure the radial clearance between the spacer and shaft. If it exceeds 0.062 mm, replace the spacer.

Checking spacer clearance on the transmission mainshaft

ASSEMBLY AND INSTALLATION

Reverse the removal and disassembly procedure and note the following:

1. When assembling the cushion rings, make certain that they are not twisted or out of position.

Installing clutch cushion rings

2. Make sure that the thrust bearings and washers are correctly positioned BEFORE installing the clutch boss.

NOTE: The thrust bearings can best be held in place by applying grease to the bearing surfaces and retaining collar.

Centrifugal Clutch

REMOVAL AND DISASSEMBLY

1. Bend in the stopper ring and lift out the ring, clutch, and friction plates.
2. Bend back the boss locknut washer tab.
3. Install the special holding tool and remove the boss locknut and clutch assembly.

INSPECTION

CLUTCH PLATE—With the assembly mounted on the shaft, measure the clearance between the stopper ring and clutch plate. Adjust the clearance to 1.0-1.2 mm (0.040-0.047 in.) by installing replacement clutch plates of an appropriate thickness.

NOTE: Clutch plates are available in 1.2 mm (0.047 in.), 1.4 mm (0.055 in), and 1.6 mm (0.063 in) thicknesses.

SPACER—Install the spacer in the primary driven gear and check it for radial play. If any play is present, replace the spacer because it will cause premature clutch wear and excessive noise.

ROLLERS AND RETAINER—Check the rollers and retainer for scratches, burrs, or rough spots. Place the rollers in the retainer grooves and roll them back and forth to make sure their movement is smooth.

ASSEMBLY AND INSTALLATION

Assembly and installation are basically a reversal of the removal and disassembly procedure. Make sure the washer, clutch plates, spacer and stopper ring are correctly positioned.

Primary Drive Gear

All Models Except YA5

REMOVAL

1. Bend back the lockwasher tab.
2. Feed a rag between the primary drive and driven gears, then loosen and remove the locknut.
3. Lift or pry off the primary gear and spacer.
NOTE: Some models also have a Woodruff key, which must be removed with the gear.

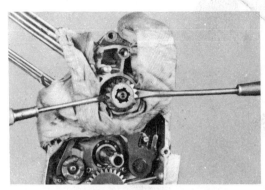

Removing the primary drive gear locknut

Removing the primary drive gear

INSPECTION

Inspect the gear teeth for signs of wear. If the primary drive gear needs replacement, the driven gear (integral with clutch housing) should also be replaced. These gears are selected in matched pairs so that gear backlash is sufficient, but not excessive. Each gear has a number stamped on it, and the total of the two serves as guide for choosing replacement parts. By installing gears whose numbers give the same total as the original set, you can be certain that the correct gear backlash is maintained.

INSTALLATION

1. Apply a small amount of grease to the chamfered end of the spacer, then position the end in the case oil seal lip.
2. Position the primary gear and Woodruff key (if so equipped) on the shaft, then install the lockwasher and locknut.

YA5

The YA5 uses a chain, rather than gears, to transmit power to the clutch. Separate one link with a chain breaker, then inspect the chain and sprockets for excessive wear. Reinstall in the reverse of removal.

Kickstarter Mechanism

1. Remove the circlip on the kickstarter idle gear.

2. Disconnect the kickstarter return spring.

3. Lift out the kickstarter assembly and return spring and remove the idle gear and washers.

4. Install by reversing the removal procedure. NOTE: Make certain the marks on the kickstarter axle and ratchet wheel are correctly aligned.

Disconnecting the kickstart return spring

Removing the kickstart idle gear circlip

Rotary Valve

Models So Equipped

REMOVAL

1. Remove attaching screws and the valve cover.

2. Remove the valve disc.

3. Drive out the valve knock pin, being careful not to damage the crankcase.

When removing the rotary-valve cover, note the position of #1 and #2 screws

Driving out the valve knock pin

INSPECTION

1. Fit the valve disc over the unit collar and check for any play or collar step wear.

Rotary-valve unit collor

Checking rotary-valve unit collar step wear

2. Check the valve cover O-ring by placing it in its groove: if the O-ring has stretched and is larger than the groove, replace it.

3. Check the crankshaft O-ring and valve disc seals for stretching or any signs of damage.

Crankshaft oil seal

INSTALLATION

When installing the rotary-valve, take care not to stretch any of the O-rings. Apply a small amount of grease to each O-ring to hold it in place, then reverse the removal procedure.

Apply grease to the rotary valve cover seals

Countershaft Sprocket

All Models

To remove the countershaft sprocket, bend back the lockwasher tab, hold the sprocket

Removing the countershaft sprocket with the magneto holding tool

with the magneto holding tool or put the transmission in gear, then remove the locknut and sprocket. Check sprocket wear as described in Maintenance.

Crankcase, Shifter and Transmission

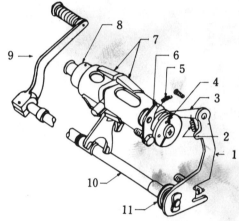

1 Gear shift arm B	6 Shift drum stopper
2 Gear shift arm	lever
spring	7 Shift fork
3 Gear shift arm A	8 Gear shift drum
4 Gear shift drum pin	9 Change pedal
5 Shift drum stopper	10 Change axle ass'y
spring	11 Gear shift spring

G6S shifter assembly. Other models are similar.

NOTE: The following procedures may vary slightly from machine to machine, depending upon model, year, etc. The basic steps are the same, however, and by carefully examining the specific engine, you can detect any differences in construction.

Rotary-Valve Singles

DISASSEMBLY

1. Remove the circlip and washer from the shifter change axle.

Removing the change axle circlip

2. Turn the engine over on the other side, then pull out the change axle and shifter arm assembly.

Pulling out the shifter shaft and arm

3. Remove the neutral stopper.
4. Remove the shift drum stopper lever and spring.

Removing the shift drum stopper

G6S shifter shaft and related parts

5. Remove all the attaching pan head screws from the left crankcase.
6. Position the connecting rod at top dead center.

7. Install the special crankcase divider tool.

Removing the case half securing screws

Installing the special case divider tool

Tapping the transmission mainshaft

8. Tighten up the divider tool bolts, making sure the tool remains parallel to the case.
9. While tightening the divider tool, alternately tap the transmission mainshaft and right half of the crankcase until it completely separates from the left half.
10. Remove the shift drum circlip, cover, and oil seal from the left crankcase.
11. Using a rubber mallet, tap out the transmission and shift drum as an assembly. Disassemble the transmission gears and shafts only if necessary.

12. Remove the crankshaft assembly with the case divider tool (see illustration).

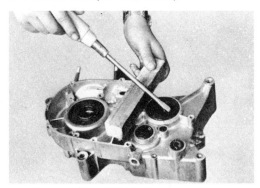

Removing the case seals

13. CAREFULLY pry out all the case seals with a straight slot screwdriver.

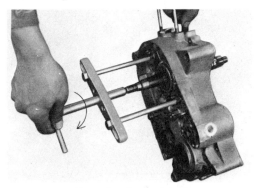

Removing the crankshaft

14. Drive out the main bearings with the special bearing tool.

INSPECTION

CONNECTING ROD—Check the connecting rod large end bearing and crankpin axial clearance by wiggling the small end and measuring its back-and-forth freeplay. Maximum is 2.0 mm; standard is 0.8–1.0 mm.

MAX. 2mm (0.079in.) OR LESS
Checking connecting rod axial play

Hold the connecting rod to one side and check the large end bearing side play with a feeler gauge. The maximum limit is 0.1–0.3 mm.

TRANSMISSION GEARS—Check the transmission gears for any burrs, broken teeth, etc., and replace any excessively worn parts.

BEARINGS—Check the transmission and main bearings as you would any other bearings. During an engine overhaul it is wise to replace the crankshaft supporting (main) bearings, as they carry most of the load and suffer the greatest wear.

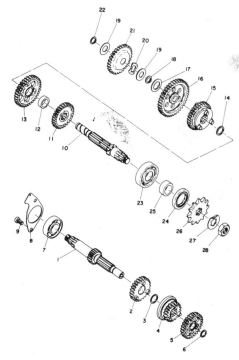

1	Main axle	15	3rd gear
2	3rd pinion gear	16	1st gear
3	Circlip	17	Shim
4	2nd pinion gear	18	Circlip
5	1st pinion gear	19	Thrust washer
6	Circlip	20	Wave washer
7	Bearing	21	Kick idler gear
8	Bearing cover plate	22	Circlip
9	Bolt	23	Bearing
10	Drive axle	24	Oil seal
11	4th gear	25	Distance collar
12	Distance collar	26	Drive sprocket
13	2nd gear	27	Lock washer
14	Circlip	28	Nut

JT1 transmission

ASSEMBLY

1. Install new oil seals with the manufacturer's mark facing outward.

2. Pack all bearings with a light weight grease and install them with the special bearing tool.

3. If the transmission cluster was disassem-

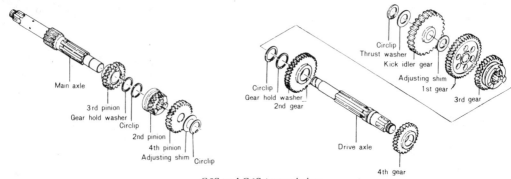

G5S and G6S transmission

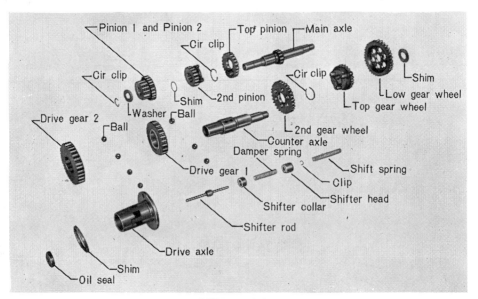

L5T transmission

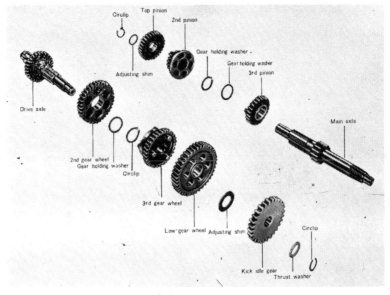

YG5T transmission

bled, make certain each gear has between 0.003 in. and 0.005 in. side play, and that the engagement dogs have AT LEAST 50% penetration into their slots. Adjustment can be achieved by adding or subtracting gear and/or drive axle shims. Use the accompanying illustrations to ensure proper shim and circlip positioning.

4. Install the crankshaft with shims, using the special crankshaft installation tool.

5. Install the transmission and shift drum assembly as one unit.

6. Clean the mating surfaces of the crankcase halves, then apply Yamaha Bond #5.

7. Make sure the transmission is NOT in first gear, then assemble the case halves.

NOTE: If the crankcase halves are assembled with the transmission in first gear, the shift forks may be bent.

90, 100, 125, 180, and 200cc Twins

DISASSEMBLY

1. Remove the shifter arm circlip and washer.
2. Turn the engine over and lift out the shifter shaft and arm assembly.
3. Remove the pan head screws on the left case half.
4. Install the crankcase dividing tool and separate the case halves as described in rotary-valve case disassembly.
5. Remove the circlip, holder and washer from the shifter drum on the left case.
6. Remove the neutral stopper mechanism.

7. Tap out the transmission and shifter as one unit.

8. Remove the crankshaft, oil seals, and main bearings as described in rotary-valve case disassembly.

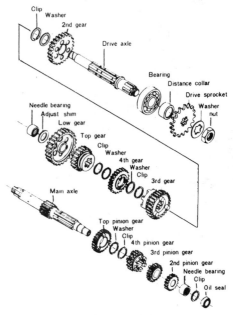

YCS1 transmission

INSPECTION AND ASSEMBLY

Inspect and assemble the crankcase, transmission, and shifter as described in rotary-valve case assembly.

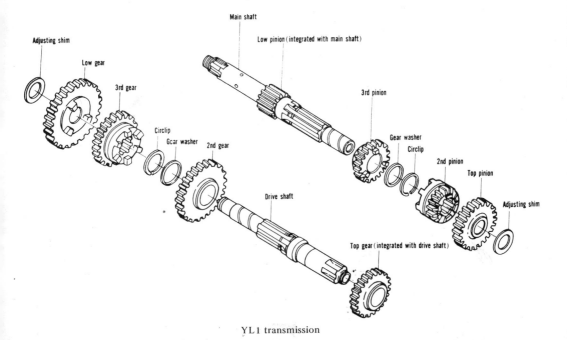

YL1 transmission

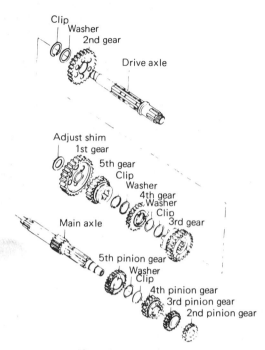

CS3 and HS1 transmission

250, 305, and 350cc Twins With Vertically Split Crankcase

DISASSEMBLY

1. Remove the shifter cover.
2. Disconnect the change link and change lever.
3. Remove the shifter cam assembly.

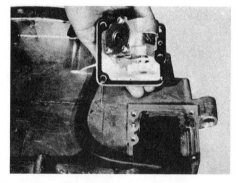

Remove the tachometer drive housing before splitting the cases

4. Remove the shifter shaft circlip and pull out the shaft.
   NOTE: Remove the external circlip first, then push the shaft inward and remove the internal circlip.
5. Remove the shift fork.
6. Remove the pan head screws on the right case half.

Removing the shifter mechanism

Shifter forks and guide bar

7. Split the case halves as previously described.
8. Remove the transmission assembly by alternately tapping drive and main axles with a rubber mallet.
9. Remove the crankshaft, oil seals, and main bearings as previously described.

INSPECTION

Inspect all parts as described in rotary-valve engine disassembly.

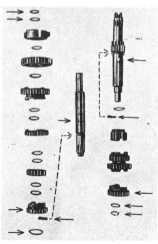

YDS3 and YM1 transmission

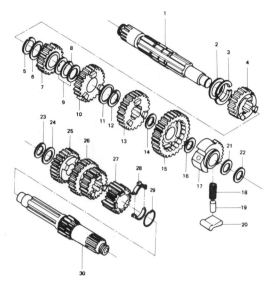

1	Drive axle	15	Kick gear
2	4th gear shim	16	Thrust washer A
3	Drive axle setting plate	17	Kick pinion gear
4	4th gear	18	Pawl spring
5	Drive axle spline circlip A	19	Kick pawl pin
6	Gear holding washer A	20	Kick pawl
7	5th gear	21	Drive axle adjust shim
8	Drive axle spline circlip	22	Drive axle adjust shim
9	Gear holding washer B	23	Main axle circlip
10	3rd gear	24	Main axle washer
11	Gear holding washer A	25	4th pinion gear
12	Drive axle spline circlip	26	3rd and 5th pinion gear
13	2nd gear	27	2nd pinion gear
14	1st gear spacer	28	2nd pinion setting plate
		29	2nd pinion holding clip
		30	Main axle

DS5, DS6 and YM2 transmission

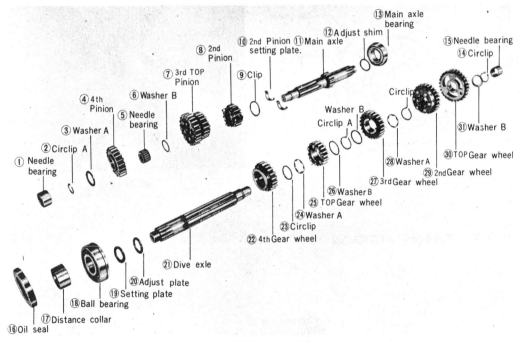

YR1 and YR2 transmission

ASSEMBLY

1. Engage the kick pinion with the kick gear.

2. Install the main axle assembly.

3. Install the drive axle assembly, meshing the gears with the main axle assembly.

4. Tap both axles into position with a rubber mallet.

5. Apply Yamaha Bond #5 to the mating surfaces of the crankcase halves, then carefully tap them together with a rubber mallet.

6. Install the pan head screws and tighten them alternately a little at a time.

7. Install the shift forks on their respective gears, then insert the shifter shaft.

8. Set the transmission in neutral position.

9. Install the shifter cam assembly.

10. Install the change link and check the shifter operation.

11. Apply Yamaha Bond #5 to the mating surfaces, then install the shifter cover and packing.

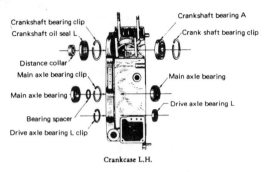

Crankcase L.H.

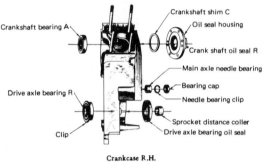

Crankcase R.H.

DS5 and DS6 bearings and oil seals. The other vertically split twins have a similar layout.

Piston Port Singles

1. Remove the tachometer drive gear circlip and gear.
2. Remove the change axle rubber boot.
3. Turn the engine over and pull out the shifter shaft assembly.
4. Remove the change lever circlip and lever.
5. Remove the neutral stopper.
6. Remove the change lever guide.
7. Remove the case pan head screws.
8. Separate the crankcase halves as previously described.
9. Remove the crankshaft, transmission/shifter assembly, oil seals, and bearings as previously described.

INSPECTION

Inspect all parts as described in rotary-valve engine disassembly.

ASSEMBLY

Assemble the crankcase as previously described and make certain that the crankshaft

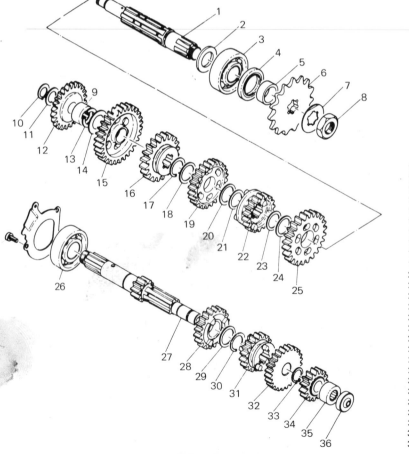

1	Drive axle
2	Spacer
3	Bearing
4	Oil seal
5	Distance collar
6	Sprocket wheel
7	Lockwasher
8	Locknut
9	Needle bearing
10	Circlip
11	Thrust washer
12	Kick idler gear
13	Circlip
14	Shim
15	1st gear
16	4th gear
17	Circlip
18	Washer
19	3rd gear
20	Washer
21	Circlip
22	5th gear
23	Circlip
24	Washer
25	2nd gear
26	Bearing
27	Main axle
28	4th pinion gear
29	Washer
30	Circlip
31	3rd pinion gear
32	5th pinion gear
33	Circlip
34	2nd pinion gear
35	Needle bearing
36	Pushrod seal

HT1, AT1 and CT1 transmission

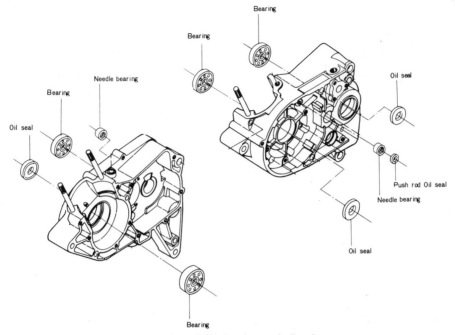

HT1, AT1 and CT1 bearings and oil seals

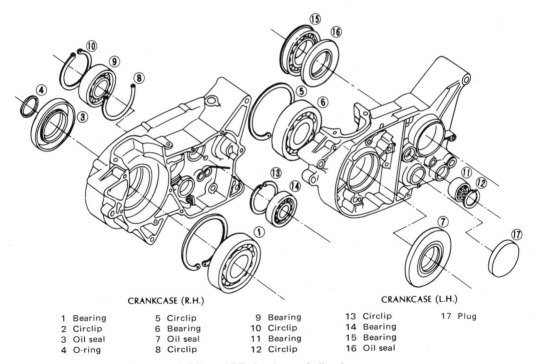

CRANKCASE (R.H.)   CRANKCASE (L.H.)

1	Bearing	5	Circlip	9	Bearing	13	Circlip	17	Plug
2	Circlip	6	Bearing	10	Circlip	14	Bearing		
3	Oil seal	7	Oil seal	11	Bearing	15	Bearing		
4	O-ring	8	Circlip	12	Circlip	16	Oil seal		

DT1 and RT1 bearings and oil seals

bearing circlip end gap is aligned with the arrows marked on both case halves.

Twins With Horizontally Split Crankcase
DISASSEMBLY

1. Remove the shifter shaft sealing boot.
2. Remove the shifter shaft circlip and shim.

3. Turn the engine over and pull out the shifter shaft assembly.

4. Remove the shift lever circlip and lever assembly.

5. Invert the engine and remove the crankcase holding bolts.

NOTE: Each holding bolt is numbered. Re-

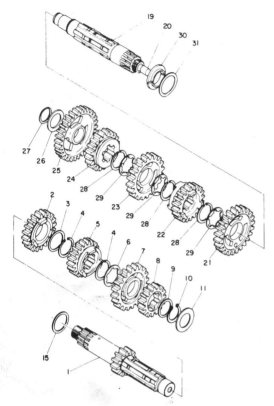

Splitting the cases

move them in descending order, beginning with the highest one.

6. Using a rubber mallet, lightly tap the case halves until they separate.

7. Remove the crankshaft by lightly tapping it with a rubber mallet.

Removing the crankshaft bearing circlips

1	Axle, main	16	Bearing
2	Gear, 4th pinion	17	Circlip
3	Washer, gear holding	18	Gear, kick pinion
4	Circlip	19	Axle, drive
5	Gear, 3rd pinion	20	Plug, blind
6	Washer, gear holding	21	Gear, 2nd wheel
7	Gear, 3rd	22	Gear, 3rd pinion
8	Gear, 2nd pinion	23	Gear, 3rd wheel
9	Washer, gear holding	24	Gear, 4th wheel
10	Circlip	25	Gear, 1st wheel
11	Shim	26	Washer, gear holding
12	Bearing	27	Circlip
13	Circlip	28	Circlip
14	Oil seal	29	Washer, gear holding
15	Shim, main axle	30	Spacer, drive axle
		31	Shim, drive axle

DT1 and RT1 transmission

8. Remove the transmission assembly.

9. Remove the shifter lever guide retaining screws and guide.

10. Remove the attaching screws and the stopper plate.

11. Pull out the guide bars, then remove the shift fork.

12. Remove the change cam stopper.

13. Remove the stopper plate circlip, then slide out the shift cam.

14. Remove the neutral switch.

15. Remove the tachometer drive gear assembly.

INSPECTION

Inspect all bearings, gears, and oil seals as previously described in rotary-valve engine disassembly.

Removing the crankcase holding bolts

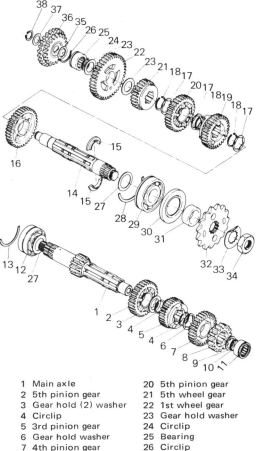

1	Main axle	20	5th pinion gear
2	5th pinion gear	21	5th wheel gear
3	Gear hold (2) washer	22	1st wheel gear
4	Circlip	23	Gear hold washer
5	3rd pinion gear	24	Circlip
6	Gear hold washer	25	Bearing
7	4th pinion gear	26	Circlip
8	2nd pinion gear	27	Drive axle shim
9	Gear hold washer	28	Circlip
10	Circlip	29	Bearing
11	Bearing	30	Oil seal
12	Bearing	31	Distance collar
13	Circlip	32	Drive sprocket
14	Drive axle	33	Lock washer
15	Drive axle spacer	34	Lock nut
16	2nd wheel gear	35	Wave washer
17	Gear hold gear	36	Idle gear ass'y
18	Circlip	37	Main axle shim
19	4th wheel gear	38	Circlip

R5 transmission

ASSEMBLY

Reverse the disassembly procedure and note the following:

1. Install the transmission main axle oil seal and circlip halves before joining upper and lower cases.

2. When installing the crankshaft, align the bearing knock pin with the hole in the lower case half.

3. Install the crankshaft bearing circlip halves and oil seal as shown in the illustrations.

4. Apply Yamaha Bond #5 to mating crankcase halves and torque the attaching bolts to the following specifications:

6 mm bolts—90 inch pounds
8 mm bolts—180 inch pounds

Tighten the bolts a little at a time in ascending order, beginning with Number 1.

XS1/XS2 SINGLE OVERHEAD CAM FOUR-STROKE

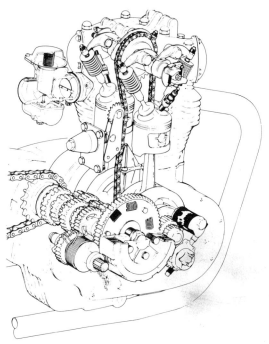

XS1/XS2 engine cutaway

This engine, derived from the Toyota 2000 GT design, is a 653cc four-stroke vertical twin. Its operation is essentially the same as any other four-stroke engine except that it utilizes a single overhead camshaft, rather than pushrods, to actuate the valves. The cam runs on four ball-bearings in the cylinder head and is driven directly by the crankshaft via an endless chain (no master link) mounted between the cylinders. An adjustable tensioner, several cushions, and a vibration damper are provided to maintain chain tension and alignment and keep noise to a minimum. The main advantage of this overhead cam arrangement is apparent in high rpm power; the valves are actuated more positively than with pushrods and, as a result, the engine will rev higher without valve float. (Valve float occurs when the piston is reciprocating faster than the valves are able to open and close). An added benefit is the system's few moving parts and their inherent reliability.

Although the XS1/XS2 powerplant resembles the traditional vertical twin in appearance, it has several unique features in addition to the over-

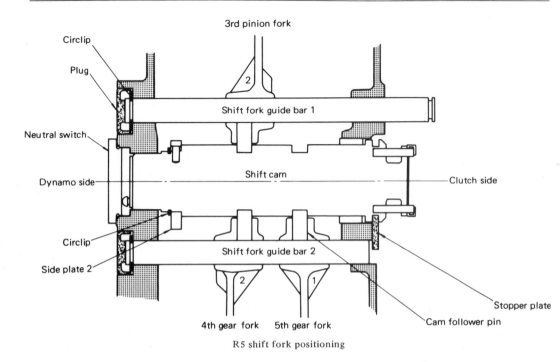

R5 shift fork positioning

head cam that make it a very advanced design in its class:

1. Constant Vacuum Carburetors—SU (Skinner's Union)-type carbs (see Fuel Systems) meter fuel mixture according to engine demand by means of vacuum diaphragms, thereby supplying just the right amount.

2. Trochoidal Oil Pump—Crankshaft driven rotary-valve type pump (see Lubrication Systems) feeds oil to the engine at a constant pressure and is more reliable than the conventional plunger-type.

3. Four Main Bearings—One ball and three roller bearings give the crankshaft strong support and ensure a long bottom end life.

4. Chrome-Plated Piston Rings—First and third piston rings are chrome-plated for longer life and better sealing.

5. Horizontally Split Crankcase—A boon to the mechanic, the unit construction case splits into upper and lower halves. This permits access to the bottom end and transmission without a complete teardown, and practically eliminates crankcase oil seepage.

6. Light Weight—Through the use of many aluminum alloy parts, the entire powerplant (including transmission) weighs in at only 135 lbs.

ENGINE REMOVAL

1. Warm up the engine and drain the oil.
2. Turn off both fuel petcocks and disconnect the fuel crossover tube.

3. Lift the seat, then remove the attaching bolts and the gas tank.

Removing the gas tank

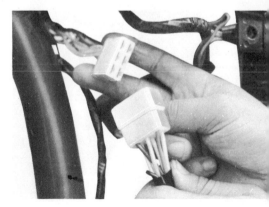

Disconnecting the alternator wiring

4. Remove both side covers.

5. Disconnect the alternator wiring harness at the center connector.

6. Disconnect both throttle cables.

7. Disconnect the air cleaner mounting bolts.

8. Disconnect the fuel balance tube and remove the carburetors.

9. Disconnect the engine breather tube.

10. Disconnect the neutral switch wire.

11. Disconnect the spark plug leads.

12. Disconnect the tachometer drive cable.

13. Disconnect ignition point and ignition switch wires.

14. Remove the horn and mounting bracket.

15. Remove the left case cover.

16. Disconnect the master link and remove the final drive chain.

17. Remove the left footrest.

18. Remove both exhaust header pipes.

19. Remove the engine top center mounting brackets.

Top engine mounting brackets

20. Remove the brake pedal.

21. Remove the engine mounting bolts in the order shown in the illustration, then lift the engine out the left side of the frame.

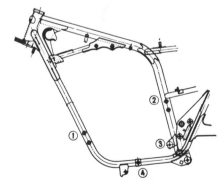

Engine mounting bolt removal sequence

ENGINE INSTALLATION

Reverse the removal procedure and torque the mounting bolts to the following specifications:

10 mm bolts—26 foot pounds
8 mm bolts—15 foot pounds

ENGINE DISASSEMBLY AND REPAIR

Follow the same basic rules for disassembly as for the two-stroke models. Remember to keep all parts separated and organized in groups. This will save you grief when time to reassemble the engine comes and make the job quicker as well.

Cylinder Head Cover

DISASSEMBLY

1. Remove the oil delivery line.

2. Remove the points, base plate, and point housing.

3. Remove the governor locknut and plate.

4. Pull the advance rod out the left (point) side.

5. Tap loose the governor unit ring nut, then slide out the unit. Also, remove the governor locating pin.

6. Remove the three attaching screws and the governor housing.

7. Remove the four tappet covers.

8. Remove the eight retainer nuts, four retainer bolts, and the head cover. Make certain to remove the nuts and bolts in the sequence shown in the illustration.

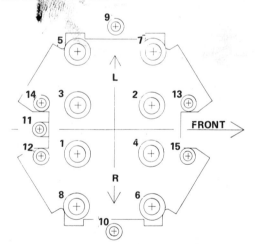

Cylinder head cover nut and bolt removal sequence

9. Remove the rocker shaft covers, sleeves, and O-rings.

10. Remove the rocker arm shafts and arms using a 6 mm extracting screw. Keep each assembly separate!

INSPECTION

Check the rocker arm for excessive wear at the two points indicated in the illustration. Look for any grooves, scratches, discoloration, or flaking of the hardened surfaces.

Removing the cylinder head cover

Rocker arm wear points

Measure the rocker shaft hole with an inside micrometer. Standard size is 15.03 mm. Also measure the rocker shaft diameter and check for step wear or discoloration. Standard diameter is 14.98 mm.

Normal shaft-to-rocker arm clearance is 0.05 mm. The maximum clearance is 0.10 mm.

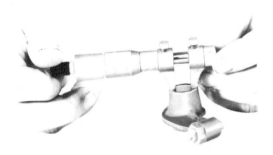

Measuring the shaft opening in the rocker arms

ASSEMBLY

Reverse the removal procedure and note the following:

1. Coat all parts with oil before assembling.
2. Make sure the rocker arms are installed with the tapped end pointed outward.

3. Coat mating head and cover surfaces with Yamaha Bond #4.

4. Make sure to coat the mounting studs with SAE 30W before installing the cover.

5. Torque 10 mm studs to 25 foot pounds, 8 mm to 14 foot pounds, and 6 mm to 7 foot pounds in the order shown in the illustration.

6. Install a new O-ring between the governor housing and head cover, and grease the oil seal lip before positioning.

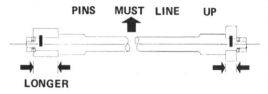

IGNITION ADVANCE ROD

Ignition advance (governor) rod installation

7. Ignition point and governor housing are identical, but can be installed in only one position.

8. Make sure no oil has leaked onto the points.

9. Make sure the point wire grommet is in good condition.

Cylinder Head

DISASSEMBLY

1. Stuff a rag under the cam chain sprocket, then break the link marked with slots and punch holes, using a chain breaker.

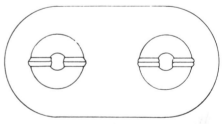

Factory marks on the cam chain joining link

NOTE: Before breaking the chain, fasten wire to the links on either side of the marked link, so that the chain won't drop into the case.

2. Remove the chain, feeding the attaching wire into the case in its place.
3. Remove the camshaft.
4. Remove the camshaft bearings.
5. Remove the carburetor manifolds.
6. Disconnect the manifold equalizer tube.
7. Remove the two attaching bolts under the

spark plugs and the screw between the intake manifold openings.

8. Lift off the cylinder head, making sure the cam chain leader wire doesn't drop into the case.

9. Using a spring compressor, remove the valve spring keepers and valve spring.

10. Remove the valve stem seal and the valve.

Removing the valve springs

INSPECTION

Check the camshaft lobes for any discoloration, pitted areas, or flaking surfaces. Measure the cam lobes as shown in the illustration and check the specified dimensions given at the end of this chapter.

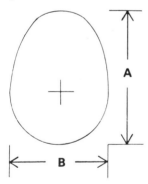

Cam lobe measuring points

Inspect the camshaft bearings for pits, rust, or chatter marks.

Check the valve stem tip for a worn spot caused by the valve adjuster. If the identation is more than 0.4–0.5 mm, grind the tip flat.

Measure the valve stem diameter and the valve guide inside diameter, then check these dimensions with those given at the end of the chapter. Also check the valve stem for straightness by rolling it along a perfectly flat surface.

Check the valve head for pits, warpage, excessive carbon build-up, etc. Using the accompanying illustrations for reference, lap or regrind the valve as necessary.

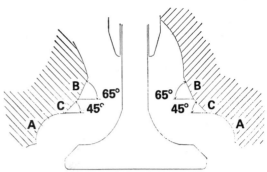

If cutting section "A" of the intake valve seat, use radiused cutter. If cutting section "A" of the exhaust valve seat, use radiused cutter.

If cutting section "B", use the 65° cutter.

If cutting section "C", use the 45° cutter.

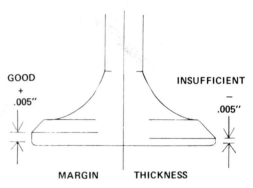

Valve margin thickness

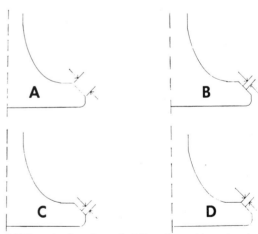

A If the valve face shows that the valve seat is centered on the valve face, but too wide; lightly use both the "R" and the 65° cutters to reduce the seat width to 1.3 mm.

B If the seat is in the middle of the valve face, but too narrow, use the 45° cutter until the width equals 1.3 mm.

C If the seat is too narrow, and right up near the valve margin; first use the "R" cutter and then the 45° cutter to get the correct seat width.

D If the seat is too narrow and down near the bottom edge of the valve face; first use the 65° cutter and then the 45° cutter.

Check the valve seat angle and measure the seat width. Correct irregularities with the necessary valve seat cutters.

After all repair work has been completed on the valve seat, install the valve and pour solvent into the intake ports. Note any signs of leakage.

Measure the valve spring free-length and check the spring pressure with a compression rate gauge.

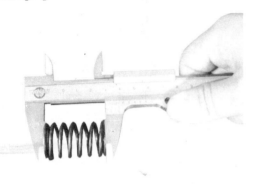

Measuring valve spring free-length

ASSEMBLY

1. Slide all the cam bearings in toward the center, then position the camshaft on the head.

2. Align the camshaft chain sprocket with the crankshaft sprocket by sliding the shaft back and forth.

3. Install a new cylinder head gasket, pull the cam chain lead wires through the cylinder head and slide the head over the studs. Install and tighten the retaining bolts and screw.

4. Position a piston at top dead center during its compression stroke.

5. Align the camshaft sprocket as shown in the illustration, then draw around and recon-

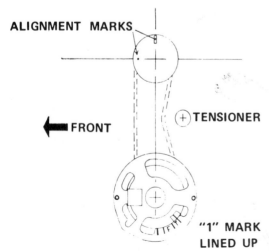

Cam chain alignment marks

nect the cam chain with a new link. Use a chain riveter to secure the new link.

6. Adjust the cam chain tensioner to remove the excess chain slack.

7. Adjust the valves to the correct clearances.

8. Mount a degree wheel to the ignition rotor lockbolt.

9. Insert a wooden dowel pin in a spark plug hole and position the degree wheel to read zero with the piston at top dead center on the compression stroke.

10. Mount a dial indicator over an intake valve adjuster.

Dial gauge installation for valve timing

11. Rotate the crankshaft counterclockwise and watch when the valve begins to open. The degree wheel should indicate 47° BTDC. If necessary, reposition the cam chain so that the valve opens at the correct point.

NOTE: Each chain link equals approximately 10° of crankshaft rotation.

Cam Chain Tensioner and Vibration Damper
REMOVAL

1. Remove the four attaching screws and the vibration damper (see illustration).

NOTE: Note the position of the two slotted screws.

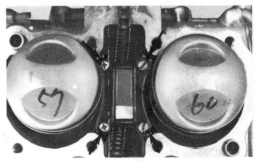

Vibration damper mounting screws

2. Remove the attaching bolts and the tensioner housing.

3. Pull out the tensioner unit.

INSTALLATION

Installation is a reversal of the removal procedure. Replace the tensioner housing gasket and apply Yamaha Bond #4 to the mating surfaces.

Cylinders and Pistons

REMOVAL, INSPECTION, AND INSTALLATION

1. Remove the oil line fitting at the cylinder base.

Removing the oil line fitting

2. Slowly lift off the cylinders and stuff some CLEAN rags into the case opening.

3. Disassemble the pistons (and related parts) and inspect the cylinders and pistons as described for two-stroke models. Ring and piston positioning data are given in the accompanying illustrations. Oversizes are given in specifications at the end of this chapter.

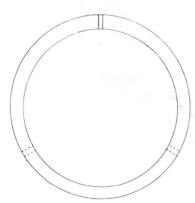

Ring gap spacing

Primary Case

DISASSEMBLY

1. Remove the attaching Allen screws and the primary case cover.

Piston size marking. Standard diameter is approximately 75mm. Number stamped on piston crown is the fractional portion of the actual size: 945 = 74.945mm.

2. Unscrew the tachometer shaft locknut.

3. Drive out the tachometer housing with a hammer and drift.

4. Lift out the tachometer gear.

5. Remove the oil pump (see Lubrication Systems).

6. Remove the oil filter.

INSTALLATION

Reverse the removal procedure.

Clutch and Primary Drive Gear

Remove, disassemble, and inspect the clutch and primary drive gear as described for the two-stroke models. Standard clutch spring free length is 38.1 mm; standard disc thickness is 3.5 mm.

Shifter and Kickstarter

REMOVAL

1. Remove the shifter shaft circlip, then turn the engine around and pull out the shaft and arm.

2. Disconnect the kickstarter return spring and pull out the assembly.

INSTALLATION

Reverse the removal procedure for installation.

Left Case Cover

DISASSEMBLY

1. Remove the attaching Allen screws and the case cover.

2. Remove the two attaching screws and the alternator stator assembly.

3. Remove the alternator rotor locknut and washer.

4. Remove the rotor with the special rotor extractor tool.

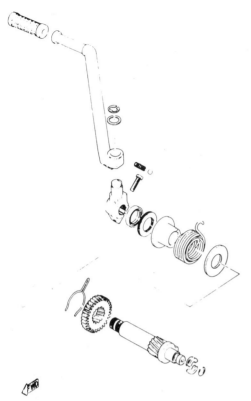

Kickstarter assembly

5. Remove the crankshaft Woodruff key.

6. Flatten the countershaft sprocket lockwasher, then put the transmission in gear, or attach a magneto holding tool, and remove the locknut and countershaft sprocket.

ASSEMBLY

Reverse the disassembly procedure and note the following:

1. When installing the kickstart mechanism, attach the return spring; rotate the kick clip until it drops into its recess, then attach the

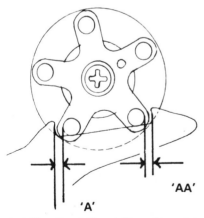

When installing the shifter shaft, make certain distances 'A' and 'AA' are equal

kickstart lever and push it 1/2 to 3/4 of the way around until the kick stopper falls into its recess. This will preload the return spring.

2. When installing the shifter mechanism, make sure dimensions "A" and "AA" are equal (see illustration).

Crankcase

DISASSEMBLY

1. Loosen and remove the numbered securing bolts in descending order, beginning with #18.

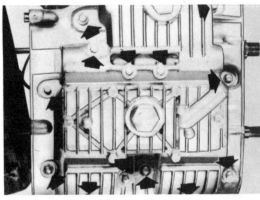

Case securing bolts

2. Tap the upper and lower case halves apart with a rubber mallet.

CAUTION: Do not tap the case cover mounting flange.

Don't hit this flange when splitting the cases!

3. Tap the transmission assembly out of the top case half with a rubber mallet.

4. Remove the neutral stopper.

5. Remove the shift drum stopper plate, then pull out the fork guide bar.

6. Remove the shift fork cam follower pin cotter keys and pins.

7. Pull out the shifter drum and remove the shift forks. Catch the cam follower rollers.

Removing the shift drum and forks

8. Tap the crankshaft out with a rubber mallet.

INSPECTION

Inspect all parts as described for the two-stroke models.

ASSEMBLY

Reverse the removal procedure and note the following:

1. Cylinder mounting studs are replaceable. Use a stud extractor for removal and install the new stud with the rounded end facing up.

2. Line up crankshaft bearing locating pins

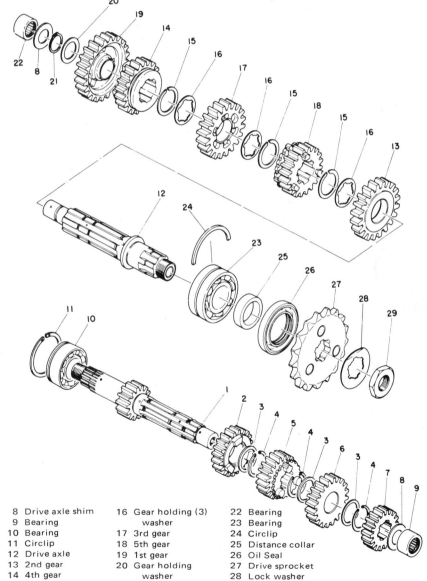

1 Main axle	8 Drive axle shim	16 Gear holding (3)
2 4th gear pinion	9 Bearing	washer
3 Gear holding (5)	10 Bearing	17 3rd gear
washer	11 Circlip	18 5th gear
4 Circlip	12 Drive axle	19 1st gear
5 3rd gear pinion	13 2nd gear	20 Gear holding
6 5th gear pinion	14 4th gear	washer
7 2nd gear pinion	15 Circlip	21 Circlip

22 Bearing
23 Bearing
24 Circlip
25 Distance collar
26 Oil Seal
27 Drive sprocket
28 Lock washer
29 Lock nut

XS1/XS2 transmission

Piston Skirt Clearance Specifications

	(mm)	(in)
U5, U5E, U5L, U7E	0.030–0.035	0.0012–0.0014
MJ2, MJ2T	0.038–0.040	0.0015–0.0016
YJl	0.038–0.040	0.0015–0.0016
*Early & Late YJ2	0.035–0.040	0.0014–0.0016
JT1, JT2	0.040–0.045	0.0016–0.0018
MG1T, YG1, YG1T, YG1K, YGS1, YGS1T	0.038–0.040	0.0015–0.0016
YG5T,G5S,G6S,G6SB,G75	0.040–0.045	0.0016–0.0018
HT1	0.040–0.050	0.0016–0.0020
HT1B, LT2	0.040–0.045	0.0016–0.0018
HS1, HS1B, LS2	0.035–0.040	0.0014–0.0016
YL2, YL2C, YL2CM	0.035–0.040	0.0014–0.0016
YL1, YL1E	0.035–0.040	0.0014–0.0016
YA5, YA6	0.040–0.045	0.0016–0.0018
AT1, AT1B, AT1C, AT2	0.040–0.045	0.0016–0.0018
YAS1(C), AS2C	0.050–0.055	0.0020–0.0022
YCS1	0.035–0.040	0.0014–0.0016
YCS1C, CS3C, CS3B, CS5	0.030–0.035	0.0012–0.0014
CT1, CT1B, CT1C, CT2	0.040–0.045	0.0016–0.0018
DT1, DT1B, DT1S, DT1C, DT1E, DS7, DT2	0.040–0.045	0.0016–0.0018
YD3, YDT1	0.050–0.055	0.0020–0.0022
YDS1, YDS2	0.055–0.060	0.0022–0.0024
*Early & Late YDS3, YDS3C	0.050–0.055	0.0020–0.0022
YDS5, DS6C, DS6B	0.035–0.040	0.0014–0.0016
YM1	0.053–0.057	0.0021–0.0023
YM2C	0.035–0.040	0.0014–0.0016
YR1	0.035–0.040	0.0014–0.0016
YR2, YR2C, R3(C)	0.030–0.035	0.0012–0.0014
R5, R5B, R5C	0.030–0.038	0.0012–0.0015
RT1, RT1B, RT2	①	0.0022–0.0024
XS1	0.050–0.060	0.0020–0.0024
XS1B, XS2	0.050–0.055	0.0020–0.0022

① RT1—0.055–0.060; RT2—0.045–0.050

and install the shaft by hand. Do not use a hammer!

3. Install the left crankshaft seal with the teflon lip facing out.

4. Lubricate all parts thoroughly before installation.

5. Replace all gaskets, seals, and cotter keys.

6. After installing the shift drum, check for proper actuation and engagement of dogs and slots.

7. Install the transmission assembly and crankshaft, then coat the case gasket with Yamaha Bond #4.

8. Torque all case securing bolts to 14 foot pounds in ascending order, beginning with bolt #1.

Clutch Specifications

	Clutch Spring Standard Lgth.		Friction Disc Standard Thick.	
	(mm)	(in)	(mm)	(in)
YJ1	34.0	1.340	3.5	0.138
YJ2	34.0	1.340	3.5	0.138
JT1, JT2	34.0	1.340	3.5	0.138
YG1, YGS1, YG5T, G5S, G6S, G6SB, G7S	27.0	1.060	3.5	0.138
HT1, HT1B, LT2	34.0	1.340	4.0	0.157
HS1, HS1B, LS2	31.5	1.229	4.0	0.157
YL2, YL2C, YL2CM, L5T, L5TA	28.2	1.302	3.5	0.138
YL1, YL1E	25.5	0.995	4.0	0.157
YA5, YA6	31.5	1.229	4.0	0.157
AT1,CT1(all),AT2,CT2	31.5	1.229	4.0	0.157
YAS1(C), AS2C	34.0	1.340	4.0	0.157
YCS1(C), CS3C, CS3B, CS5	34.0	1.340	4.0	0.157
DT1 (all), DT2	36.4	1.433	3.0	0.118
YD3, YDT1, YDS1, YDS2				
YDS3(C), YM1	25.5	0.995	4.3	0.168
YDS5, YM2(C)	25.5	0.995	3.0	0.118
DS6C, DS6B	44.0	1.716	3.0	0.118
YR1, YR2(C), R3(C)	36.4	1.433	3.0	0.118
R5, R5B, DS7, R5C	36.0	1.404	3.0	0.118
RT1, RT1B, RT2	36.4	1.433	3.0	0.118

XS1/XS2 Piston Ring Specifications

TOP AND MIDDLE RINGS		BOTTOM RING RAILS			RING GAP		
Size (mm)	Mark	Size		Color		Standard Gap (mm)	Wear Limit
Standard	None	Standard		Blue (1 mark)	Compression Ring	.2–.4	.8
Oversize 1st	25	Oversize 1st	25 (0.25 mm)	Blue (2 marks)			
2nd	50	2nd	50 (0.50 mm)	Red (1 mark)	Wiper Ring	.2–.4	.8
3rd	75	3rd	75 (0.75 mm)	Red (2 marks)	Oil Control (Rails)	.3–.6	1.0
4th	100	4th	100 (1.0 mm)	Yellow (1 mark)			

XS1/XS2 Cam Lobe Specifications

	Cam Lift (A)		Base Circle Diameter (B)	
	Standard Value	Wear Limit	Standard Value	Wear Limit
Intake	39.63 ± 0.05	39.39	32.19 ± 0.05	32.12
Exhaust	39.36 ± 0.05	39.39	32.24 ± 0.05	32.17

XS1/XS2 Valve Seat Specifications

Standard Width	Wear Limit
1.3 mm (.051 in)	2.0 mm (.078 in)

XS1/XS2 Valve Guide Specifications

			Original Clearance	Replacement Clearance
Intake	Valve Guide ID	8.010–8.019mm	.020–.044mm	.100mm
	Valve Stem OD	7.975–7.790mm		
Exhaust	Valve Guide ID	8.010–8.019mm	.035–.059mm	.120mm
	Valve Stem OD	7.960–7.975mm		

XS1/XS2 Valve Spring Specifications

	Outer	Inner
Diameter of Wire	4.5mm	2.9mm
Direction of Winding	Right Hand	Left Hand
Total Windings	6.0	7.25
Free Length	41.8mm	41.0mm
Installed Length (Valve Closed)	37mm	35mm
Installed Pressure	20.1kg (44 lbs)	9.7kg (20 lbs)
Compressed Length (Valve Open) Measured without collar	27.8mm	25.8mm
Compressed Pressure	60.0kg (132 lbs)	25kg (55 lbs)

All measurements ± three percent

Torque Specifications

size	kg/m	ft lbs	in lbs
6mm	1.0	7	90
7mm	1.5	11	135
8mm	2.0	15	180
10mm	3.5–4.0	26–29	300–350
12mm	4.0–4.5	29–33	350–400
14mm	4.5–5.0	33–37	400–450
17mm	5.8–7.0	40–50	500–600

5 ● Lubrication Systems

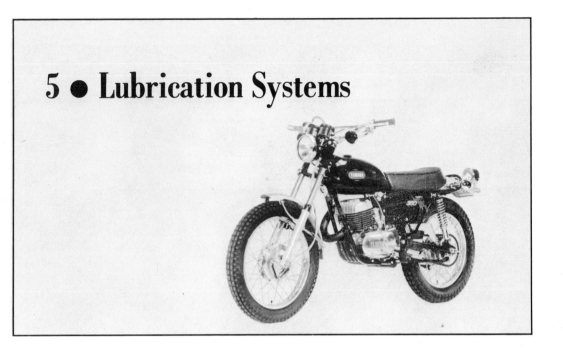

Two-Stroke Models

Autolube

The original oil-injected two-stroke engines were developed during the 1920s by two British manufacturers—Scott and Villiers. The Scott engine used a mechanically-driven oil pump, but Villiers used a needle valve mechanism operated by crankcase compression. Then in the 1930s, a third British firm, Velocette, added yet another approach to the oil-injection idea: a mechanically-driven, THROTTLE-CONTROLLED oil pump.

But, as was the case with many other ideas of that time, further development was shelved due to the war and limited materials, machining equipment, etc. Then in 1963, when the future of two-stroke motorcycles looked the gloomiest, the Yamaha Technical Research Institute applied modern techniques to the basic oil-injection concept, and came up with Autolube. This new system suceeded in alleviating the problems that surely would have caused the downfall of two-stroke motorcycles: oil/gas premixing, heavy oil consumption, billowing clouds of exhaust smoke, and the constant threat of either plug fouling or piston seizure.

DESCRIPTION

The Autolube system includes an oil reservoir, oil feed line, oil pump, and oil delivery lines. The pump is of the plunger type and is driven by the crankshaft or clutch (early models) through reduction gears. The amount of oil fed to the crankcase delivery line is determined by two variables—the speed of plunger operation and the length of plunger stroke. These variables are set by the engine rpm and the degree of throttle opening, respectively. The pump effectively meters the amount of oil according to engine speed and load and, as a result, no more and no less than the required amount is consumed. The pump also houses a check valve that keeps the oil output pressure constant and seals the delivery line when the engine is not operating.

PUMP REPAIR

The factory advises against attempting to disassemble and repair the oil pump. The internal parts are machined to very exacting tolerances and it is highly unlikely that the pump could be reassembled to factory specifications. In addition to this, Autolube pump failure is VERY seldom due to internal malfunction.

PUMP ADJUSTMENT

See the Tune-up Chapter.

PUMP BLEEDING

The oil pump must be bled of all air whenever any supply or delivery lines are disconnected or the oil tank has run dry.

1. Remove the bleeder bolt.
2. Turn the starter plate in the direction indicated by the arrow on the plate.
3. Keep turning the plate until the bleeder hole spurts oil only (i.e. no air bubbles).

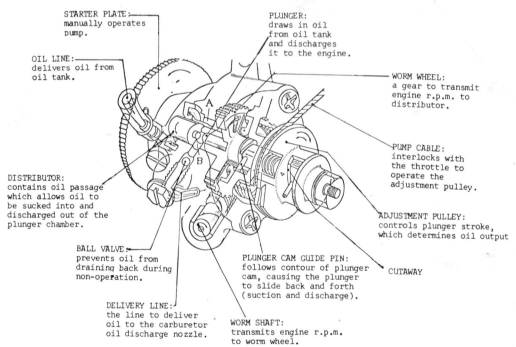

STARTER PLATE:
manually operates
pump.

PLUNGER:
draws in oil
from oil tank
and discharges
it to the engine.

OIL LINE:
delivers oil from
oil tank.

WORM WHEEL:
a gear to transmit
engine r.p.m. to
distributor.

DISTRIBUTOR:
contains oil passage
which allows oil to
be sucked into and
discharged out of the
plunger chamber.

PUMP CABLE:
interlocks with
the throttle to
operate the
adjustment pulley.

ADJUSTMENT PULLEY:
controls plunger stroke,
which determines oil output

BALL VALVE:
prevents oil from
draining back during
non-operation.

PLUNGER CAM GUIDE PIN:
follows contour of plunger
cam, causing the plunger
to slide back and forth
(suction and discharge).

CUTAWAY

DELIVERY LINE:
the line to deliver
oil to the carburetor
oil discharge nozzle.

WORM SHAFT:
transmits engine r.p.m.
to worm wheel.

Autolube pump cutaway

NOTE: This operation will be much easier if you hold the throttle wide open while turning the starter plate.

4. Reinstall the bleeder bolt.

5. If the pump is being bled as part of engine reassembly after major repairs, keep in mind that the crankcase is probably stone dry. When you start the engine, let it idle for awhile and hold the oil pump cable full open for a few seconds. This will provide the moving parts

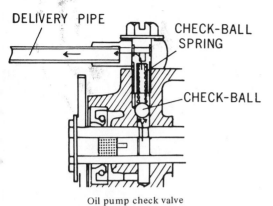

Oil pump check valve

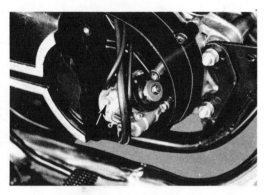

Arrow indicates the bleeder bolt

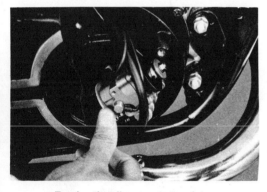

Turning the oil pump starter plate

with extra lubrication until the normal oil film is built up.

PUMP OUTPUT CHECK
(1969, '70, and '71 MODELS ONLY)

The delivery output of the oil pump should be measured when the pump is suspected as the cause of a problem and after the more common sources have been checked (see Autolube Troubleshooting).

Needed for this operation are: a laboratory tube graduated in cubic centimeters, an extra oil pump delivery line, strong fingers, and fifteen minutes of unshakeable patience.

NOTE: This check can be performed with the pump mounted in the bike or on the bench.

1. Cut off one end of the extra delivery line and slide it over the end of the graduated tube (see illustration).

2. Disconnect the oil pump delivery line banjo bolt and connect the measuring tube assembly in its place.

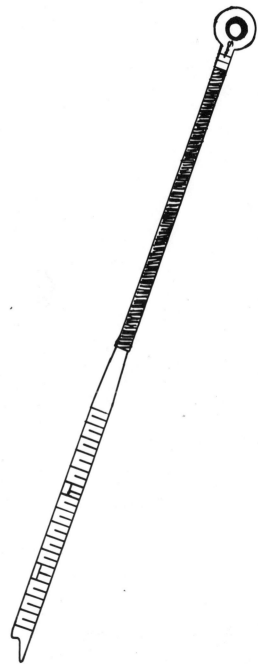

Oil pump output measuring rig

NOTE: On twins, you can measure only one output at a time.

3. Make sure there is some oil in the reservoir, then set the pump at minimum or maximum plunger stroke.

NOTE: When checking maximum output, turn the pump pulley so that the ramp moves along the guide pin to the maximum position. DO NOT PUSH the pulley straight into position because the plunger stroke may then be longer than when actuated by the cable.

4. Turn the starter pulley 200 revolutions and note the amount of oil in the graduated tube. Check this figure with the specified output.

5. If there is still some doubt, reset the pump at the maximum or minimum output position (whichever was not used the first time) and repeat the operation.

XS1/XS2

The XS1/XS2 has a wet sump type pressure-fed lubrication system which consists of a trochoidal oil pump, a strainer screen, an oil filter, case delivery passages, and rocker arm feed lines. Oil from the crankcase is sucked through the strainer, then pumped through the wire mesh filter into the delivery passages and lines.

Direct lubrication is provided to the following:

1. Crankshaft main bearings.

Autolube Pump Output

	Minimum Stroke (cc @ 200 rev)	Maximum Stroke (cc @ 200 rev)
JT1, G5S, G6S, G6SB, HT1, HT1B, L5T, L5TA	0.50–0.63	4.65–5.15
HS1, HS1B, YL1/E, AS2C	0.50–0.63	4.20–4.80
CS1C, CS3B, CS3C, DS6B, DS6C, R2/C, R3, R5, R5B	0.50–0.63	5.15–5.70
AT1, AT1B, AT1C, CT1, CT1B, CT1C	0.50–0.63	8.80–9.76
DT1B, DT1C, DT1E, RT1 (late), RT1B	0.95–1.19	8.80–9.76
RT1 (early)	1.19–1.44	9.10–10.05

2. Connecting rod large end bearings.
3. Transmission mainshaft.
4. Clutch bearing.
5. Shift fork guide bar.
6. Rocker arms.

Oil splash in the crankcase lubricates the:
1. Crankshaft.
2. Connecting rod small-end bearings.
3. Camshaft drive chain.
4. Piston and cylinder walls.
5. Transmission gears and driving shaft.
6. Primary drive gears.

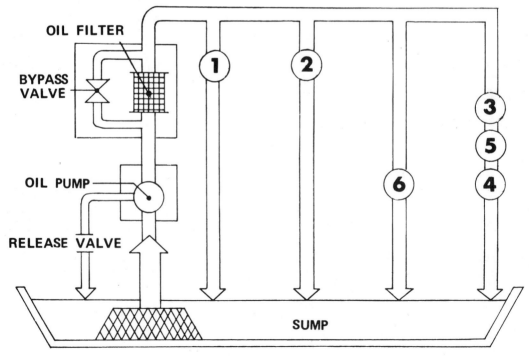

XS1/XS2 direct lubrication system. See text for number key

1 Pump housing   3 Inner rotor
2 Outer rotor   4 Drive shaft

PUMP DESCRIPTION

The pump is a rotary-valve design, rather than the conventional plunger-type, and is driven directly by the crankshaft through a straight-cut reduction gear. The pump consists mainly of a shaft, housing, and two spinning rotors. One of the rotors is mounted on the end of the shaft and has four rounded points; the other is freewheeling, has five rounded indentations and surrounds the first. As the inner rotor turns, it causes the outer rotor to spin also, but at a different speed. This, in turn, causes a constantly varying gap between the inner and outer rotors and results in a four-stage constant pressure output (see illustration).

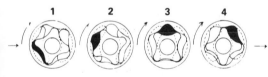

Oil pumping stages

The pump is also equipped with a ball and spring relief valve that, when open, detours oil flow directly back to the sump supply. This valve is provided in case of excessive back-pressure in the delivery passages.

PUMP REMOVAL

1. Remove the tachometer shaft locknut, then drive out the tachometer housing with a punch.
2. Remove the tachometer gear, washer, and O-ring.

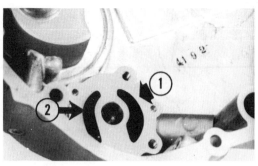

1 Case inlet cavity   2 Case outlet cavity

3. Remove the oil pump gear and Woodruff key.
4. Remove the pump housing retaining screws and, while tapping the housing with a soft-faced hammer, lift out the pump.

PUMP INSTALLATION

Installation of the oil pump is basically a reversal of the removal procedure with the addition of the following:
1. Make sure the notches in the inner rotor and drive shaft are correctly aligned.
2. Install the pump as a unit, using the locating pin provided for alignment.

Oil pump locating pin and hole

3. Replace the tachometer drive gear O-ring.

PUMP REPAIRS

There isn't much that can go wrong in the XS1/XS2 oil pump, but should some dirt get lodged between the rotors, the tachometer would cease functioning before too much damage could be done. Other than this rare occurrence, however, the oil pump is virtually maintenance and repair free.

6 ● Fuel Systems

Two-Stroke Models

Carburetors

The carburetors used on all Yamaha two-stroke engines are the Amal-type. They serve the function of mixing, metering, atomizing and delivering the fuel/air mixture to the crankcase.

Ideally, carburetors supply a ratio of fuel and air to provide the most thorough combustion. This ideal ratio is generally accepted as being one part fuel to fifteen parts air—by weight. Such a mixture allows the fuel to mix completely with the oxygen and, therefore, be completely burnt. In the case of two-stroke engines, however, a slightly rich ratio is recommended because the excess fuel aids in cooling the combustion chamber.

OPERATION

Basically, a carburetor consists of a float chamber, fuel nozzle, and a Venturi tube. Fuel from the gas tank flows into the float chamber, where it is monitored by an air-filled float. This float has a small needle at the top, and when the fuel has reached a preset level, it seals off the fuel entrance passage and prevents overfilling. Then, as the fuel is consumed by the engine, the float and float needle drop down, allowing more fuel from the gas tank to bring the level back to normal.

The fuel nozzle, or jet, is connected to the float chamber and positioned so that its top

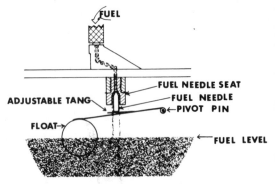

Float chamber arrangement

opening is just a little bit higher than the fuel level in the float chamber. This keeps fuel always present in the jet, but never free-flowing out of it.

At the top opening of the fuel jet is the venturi, or carburetor throat. The venturi is a passage that is narrower in the center than at the ends. When air rushes through it, a low pressure area is created in the narrow section, and in an effort to equalize this low pressure, fuel is forced, or sucked, into the venturi passage.

Of course, the modern Mikuni carburetors used on Yamaha two-strokes aren't quite that simple. The basic carburetor described above makes no provisions for throttle control, cold weather starting, or varying engine needs under special conditions.

The operation of a Mikuni carburetor can best be described by dividing it into five circuits and the parts that control each one.

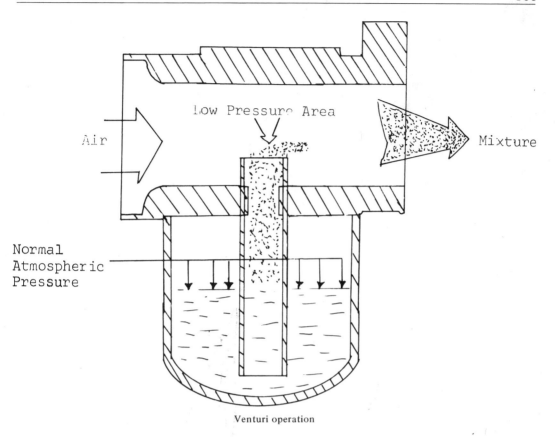

Venturi operation

STARTING CIRCUIT—When the engine is cold, it needs a slightly richer fuel mixture than it does at normal operating temperatures. The Mikuni carburetor supplies this rich mixture through a circuit that is completely independent from the rest of the carburetor parts.

Fuel and air passages are drilled directly into a starter circuit mixing chamber; another passage leads directly to the venturi. The system is activated when the starter lever is pushed down: this lifts a small plunger and allows fuel and air to enter the mixing chamber, where crankcase suction then draws the mixture through the venturi and into the engine. When the lever is raised, the plunger drops, blocking off the fuel and air passages and eliminating the starter circuit mixture supply.

IDLE CIRCUIT (0-1/8 Throttle Opening)— At idle, under normal operating conditions, the engine requires very little fuel and air. It does require, however, more accurate metering than pure venturi action can provide while the engine is still turning over slowly and intake air velocity is low.

The circuit consists of a pilot jet air passage, pilot jet fuel passage and the throttle slide (see illustration). Fuel is provided from the float chamber through the pilot jet and passage; air is

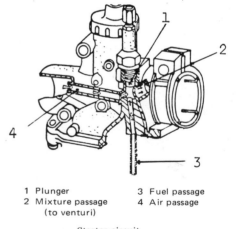

1 Plunger	3 Fuel passage
2 Mixture passage	4 Air passage
(to venturi)	

Starter circuit

supplied mainly by the venturi, but also through the pilot air jet and passage. The pilot air jet serves a very important function, even though it doesn't provide most of the air for mixing. It is actually an adjustable needle valve, and the amount of air it lets through can be changed to compensate for atmospheric conditions.

In operation, crankcase suction creates a low-pressure area behind the throttle slide. To equalize this low pressure, air rushes through

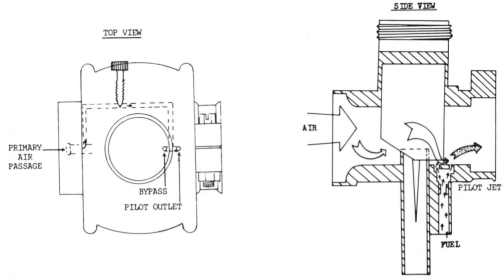

Idle circuit

the pilot air passage and mixes with the fuel from the pilot fuel passage. The incoming air under the throttle slide atomizes and delivers the mixture to the crankcase.

NOTE: The slide cutaway (see illustration) lets air fill the area around the main and needle jets so that raw fuel isn't drawn into the low-pressure area behind the slide.

LOW-SPEED CIRCUIT (1/8-1/4 Throttle Opening)—This circuit uses the same components as the Idle Circuit, but the throttle slide is now lifted and air velocity through the venturi

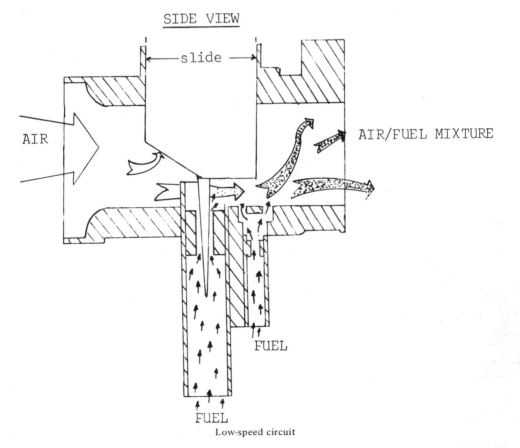

Low-speed circuit

is sufficient to draw some fuel through the main and needle jets (see illustration). Although more air is rushing under the throttle slide, the amount of slide cutaway still limits the amount of venturi action.

MID-RANGE CIRCUIT (1/4–3/4 Throttle Opening)—In this circuit, air is supplied by two sources: the venturi and the primary air passage. Fuel is supplied by the float chamber and controlled by the needle jet and jet needle. Although they sound confusing, there's nothing really complicated about these parts. The needle jet is located above the main jet and works in conjunction with the jet needle, which is suspended from the throttle slide (see illustration). The primary air passage is drilled from

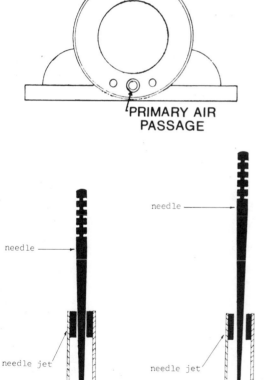

PRIMARY AIR PASSAGE

Needle jet and jet needle operation

the very front of the venturi to the needle jet (usually sharing its entrance with the pilot air passage). The air from this passage serves to aid in the atomization of the fuel being drawn through the needle jet.

In operation, the needle jet and jet needle

work together to supply a corresponding amount of fuel as the throttle slide raises and venturi action takes effect. The jet needle is tapered so that, as it is lifted, more fuel is allowed to pass through the needle jet.

HIGH-SPEED CIRCUIT (3/4–Full Throttle) —This circuit is close to that described for the basic carburetor. The jet needle has lifted out of the needle jet and, therefore, no longer controls the amount of fuel and the throttle slide has raised high enough so that it has minimal control over the amount of air intake.

Venturi action takes over completely. The amount of air sucked into the crankcase is determined by the venturi diameter, and the amount of fuel supplied for mixing is determined by the size of the main jet. The only other component that still has a significant effect is the primary air passage which continues to aid fuel atomization.

DISASSEMBLY

1. Remove the four bottom float bowl screws.
2. Remove the float bowl.
3. Push out the float pin and remove the float, noting its position.
4. Remove the starter jet mechanism.
5. Remove the fuel needle and unscrew the fuel needle seat.
6. Remove the main jet.
7. Remove the needle jet.

NOTE: Mikuni carburetors have two types of needle jets—one screws into position, the other is held in place by a small clip.

8. Remove the pilot jet with a small flat head screwdriver.

CLEANING

Clean all parts in solvent, then blow dry with compressed air. Make sure all the jets are free from obstruction.

ASSEMBLY

Assemble the carburetor in the reverse order of disassembly.

FLOAT LEVEL ADJUSTMENT

NOTE: Float level is preset at the factory. An adjustment should be necessary only after installing a new float or when the adjustable tang has been bent.

INTERCONNECTED FLOAT TYPE (SC)

1. Turn the carburetor upside-down and tilt it until the float pivots up against the fuel inlet passage needle.
2. Make certain the fuel inlet needle is seated,

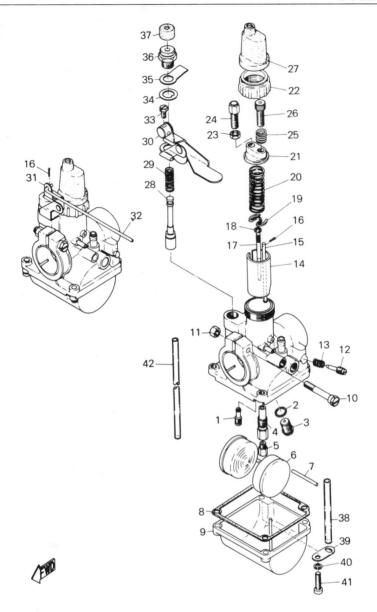

1 Pilot jet	23 Wire adjusting nut
2 Valve seat washer	23 Wire adjusting nut
3 Valve seat assembly	24 Wire adjusting screw
4 Main nozzle	25 Throttle stop spring
5 Main jet	26 Throttle screw
6 Float	27 Cap
7 Float pin	28 Starter plunger
8 Float chamber gasket	29 Plunger spring
9 Float chamber body	30 Starter lever (left)
10 Body fitting screw	31 Starter lever (right)
11 Nut	32 Starter lever rod
12 Air adjusting screw	33 Rod screw
13 Air adjusting spring	34 Starter lever washer
14 Throttle valve	35 Starter lever plate
15 Throttle bar	36 Plunger cap
16 Cotter pin	37 Plunger cap cover
17 Needle	38 Air vent pipe*
18 Clip	39 Plate
19 Spring seat	40 Spring washer
20 Throttle valve spring	41 Panhead screw
21 Mixing chamber top	42 Overflow pipe

SC type Mikuni carburetor

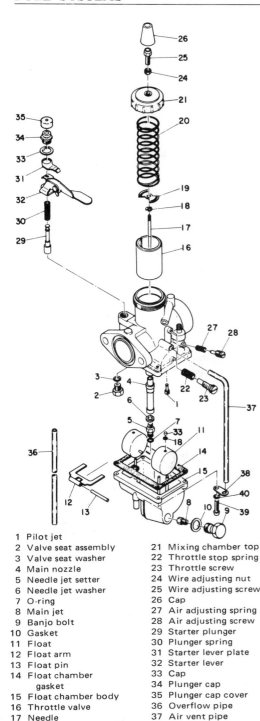

4. If an adjustment is necessary to meet specifications, bend the tang, not the float arm.

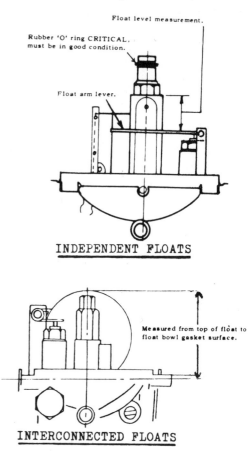

Float level measurement.

Rubber 'O' ring CRITICAL, must be in good condition.

Float arm lever.

INDEPENDENT FLOATS

Measured from top of float to float bowl gasket surface.

INTERCONNECTED FLOATS

Float level adjustment

1 Pilot jet	21 Mixing chamber top
2 Valve seat assembly	22 Throttle stop spring
3 Valve seat washer	23 Throttle screw
4 Main nozzle	24 Wire adjusting nut
5 Needle jet setter	25 Wire adjusting screw
6 Needle jet washer	26 Cap
7 O-ring	27 Air adjusting spring
8 Main jet	28 Air adjusting screw
9 Banjo bolt	29 Starter plunger
10 Gasket	30 Plunger spring
11 Float	31 Starter lever plate
12 Float arm	32 Starter lever
13 Float pin	33 Cap
14 Float chamber gasket	34 Plunger cap
15 Float chamber body	35 Plunger cap cover
16 Throttle valve	36 Overflow pipe
17 Needle	37 Air vent pipe
18 Clip	38 Plate
19 Spring seat	39 Pan head screw
20 Throttle valve spring	40 Spring washer

SH type Mikuni carburetor

then let it spring back until the adjustable tang is lightly touching it.

3. Measure the distance from the float bowl gasket surface to the top of the float.

INDEPENDENT FLOAT TYPE (SH)

1. Remove the float bowl and turn the carburetor upside-down.

2. Measure the distance from the needle jet housing surface to each of the float arms.

3. If necessary, bend the adjustable tang to achieve the proper clearance.

SPECIFICATIONS AND DESIGNATIONS

Carburetor parts are given letter and/or number designations according to their size, taper, etc. Explanations for these designations as applied to Mikuni carburetors are given below.

MAIN JET (M.J.)—Main jet size on Mikuni carburetors indicates the amount of fuel flow in cubic centimeters during one minute. For example, a size 100 indicates a fuel flow of 100 cc/minute.

NEEDLE JET (N.J.)—The needle jet inner diameter is given as a coded letter and number. A-0, for example, indicates an inside diameter of 1.9 mm. The letter determines the size in increments of 0.050 mm; the number gives in-between sizes in steps of 0.005 mm. Therefore, A-2 has an inside diameter of 1.910 mm, B-0 has an inside diameter of 1.950, etc.

JET NEEDLE (J.N.)–The first number indicates the overall length of the needle. 3 is 30–40 mm, 4 is 40–50 mm, etc.

The letter indicates the needle taper. A is $0° 15'$, B is $0° 30'$, and so on, in increments of $15'$. The next letter and/or number(s) identify the manufacturer.

The last number indicates the standard groove for the clip: 1 is the top groove, 2 is the second from the top, and so on, through 5.

THROTTLE VALVE CUTAWAY (C.A.)– The degree of throttle valve cutaway is indicated by a number. The larger the number, the greater the cutaway size.

PILOT JET (P.J.)–The pilot jet number indicates the amount of fuel flow (in cubic centimeters) per minute.

STARTER JET (S.J.)–The starter jet number indicates fuel flow in cc/minute.

Gas Tank

The gas tank is usually a maintenance-free item. However, if the bike has been stored for a considerable time and water has condensed inside, you may be faced with a rust problem.

Rust removal can be a pretty tedious job, but there are several shortcuts that can make it less difficult. One of these is the "fistful" of nuts and bolts method:

1. Remove the fuel petcock and plug the tank hole.

2. Fill the tank about 1/4 full of gasoline.

3. Add a few handfuls of nuts, bolts and washers.

4. Put the gas cap back on, then shake the tank vigorously until you can't hold it any longer.

5. Remove the petcock hole plug and drain the gas.

Repeat the above once or twice and, after removing the nuts and bolts, flush the tank several times with fresh fuel.

FUEL PETCOCK

If you experience any fuel delivery problems, first check the gas tank vent, then the fuel petcock. Any sediment, water, etc., in the gas tank will eventually settle in the petcock filter or bowl. Remove the petcock, disassemble it, wash the filter in solvent, then blow everything dry with compressed air and reinstall.

XS1/XS2

Carburetors

The 650cc XS1/XS2 uses twin Mikuni constant-vacuum carburetors. Air flow through the venturi is determined by throttle slide position as in the Amal-type Mikunis, but is operated by intake manifold vacuum, rather than by a cable connected to the twist grip.

OPERATION

NOTE: Use the illustrations for reference.

The vacuum piston (1) fits into the carburetor bore, and a rubber diaphragm (2), attached to the piston top and housing, divides the top of the carburetor into two chambers: a vacuum chamber (3), above the diaphragm, and an atmospheric chamber (4), below the diaphragm.

As air is sucked through the venturi by engine vacuum, it creates a low pressure area at the back of the vacuum piston. A drilled passage through the piston (5) allows this low-pressure air to fill the vacuum chamber above the diaphragm; since the area below the diaphragm is at atmospheric pressure, the diaphragm and piston lift to compensate for the pressure differential until the combination of the atmospheric pressure and the tension of the piston spring (6) equalize the difference.

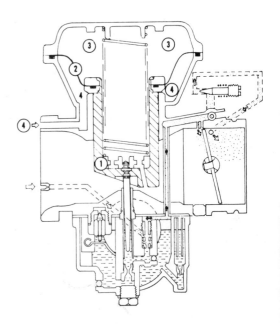

The velocity of incoming air through the venturi is controlled by the butterfly valve, which is operated by the throttle twist grip via cable. As the valve opens, air velocity increases, caus-

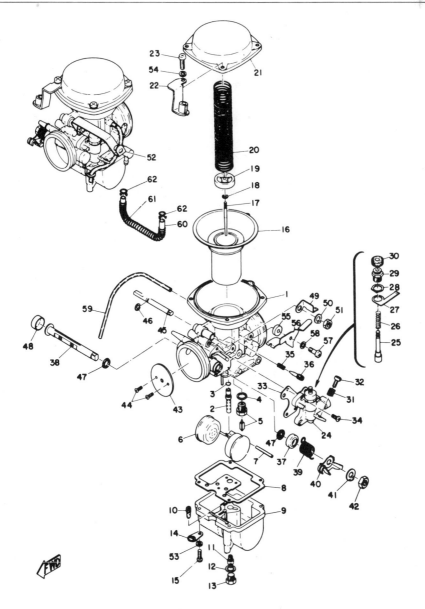

1 Body assembly (left)	22 Throttle bracket (left)	43 Throttle valve
2 Main nozzle	23 Pan head screw	44 Oval head screw
3 O-ring	24 Starter body assembly	45 Starter shaft
4 Washer	25 Starter plunger	46 Clip
5 Valve seat assembly	26 Plunger spring	47 Seal
6 Float	27 Set lever starter spring	48 Cap
7 Float pin	28 Washer	49 Starter lever
8 Float chamber packing	29 Plunger cap	50 Washer
9 Float chamber body	30 Plunger cap cover	51 Nut
10 Pilot jet	31 Throttle stop spring	52 Connector lever
11 Main jet	32 Throttle stop screw	53 Spring washer
12 Washer	33 Starter packing	54 Spring washer
13 Plug screw	34 Flat head screw	55 Ring
14 Plate	35 Pilot screw spring	56 Lever assembly
15 Pan head screw	36 Pilot screw	57 Pan head screw
16 Diaphragm assembly	37 Cap	58 Spring washer
17 Needle	38 Throttle assembly shaft	59 Overflow pipe
18 Clip	39 Throttle spring	60 Fuel pipe
19 Set needle plate	40 Throttle lever	61 Spring
20 Diaphragm spring	41 Washer	62 Pipe clip
21 Diaphragm cover	42 Nut	

Mikuni BS38 carburetor

ing a greater pressure drop in the vacuum chamber. This in turn causes the diaphragm and piston to lift higher.

Other than the use of the diaphragm and vacuum piston, the constant vacuum type carburetor operates similarly to the Amal-type.

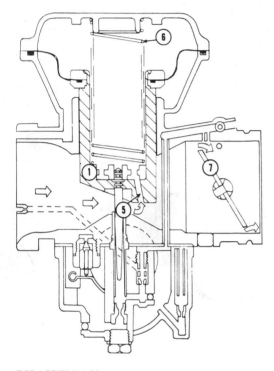

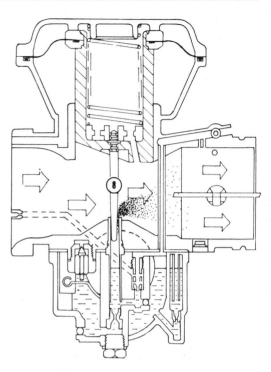

DISASSEMBLY

1. Remove the attaching screws and the vacuum chamber cover.

2. Remove the spring needle retainer, jet needle, and vacuum piston.

3. Remove the attaching screws, the starter jet housing, and gasket.

4. Remove the attaching screws and the float bowl.

5. Remove the cover screw, main jet, and pilot jet.

6. Turn the carburetor upside-down and remove the float and float pivot pin.

7. Remove the float valve.

8. Remove the needle jet.

CLEANING

Clean all parts in solvent then blow them dry with compressed air. Make sure that all jets are free from obstruction.

ASSEMBLY—Reverse the removal procedure and replace all gaskets.

GAS TANK AND FUEL PETCOCK—See the section on two-stroke models if cleaning is necessary.

XS1/XS2 Carburetor Specifications

Type (BS38 Mikuni)*	W1 ①	E2 ②	E3 ③	E4 ④
Main Jet (M.J.)	130	130	130	130
Pilot Jet (P.J.)	45	45	42.6	42.5
Pilot Outlet (P.O.)	0.8	0.8	0.7	—
Pilot Bypass #1 (P.B.1)	1.0	1.0	0.8	—
Pilot Bypass #2 (P.B.2)	0.6	0.6	1.0	—
Air Jet (A.J.)	1.0	1.0	1.2	—
Needle Jet (N.J.)	Z-6	Z-6	Z-6	Z-6
Jet Needle (J.N.)	4JN19-4	4JN19-4	4JN19-4	4J
Air Screw (A.S.)	½	1	1	¾
Starter Jet (S.J.)	0.6	0.6	0.6	0.7
Float Level (F.L.) (mm)	25	25	25	25
Air Vent (A.V.)	2.5	3.0	4.0	—

① Engine nos. 00101–02514.

② Engine nos. 02515–03628.

③ Engine nos. 03629–100101.

* Types W1 and E2 are interchangeable; E3 carburetors must be used as a set.

④ Engine nos. 100101–

Two-Stroke Carburetor Specifications

	Type (Mikuni)	Main Jet (M.J.)	Air Jet (A.J.)	Needle Jet (N.J.)	Jet Needle (J.N.)	Cut Away (C.A.)	Pilot Jet (P.J.)	Air Screw (A.S.)	Starter Jet (S.J.)	Flat Level ② (F.L.)
U7E	VM15SC	100	2.4	E-8	3G9-3	2.5	12.5	1¾	25	22.5
Late YJ2	VM16	60	—	E-0	3D1-3	1.5	17.5	1½	15	23
JT1, JT2	Y16P	86	0.7	2.085	032-2	1.5	38.0	1½	50	—
YG1, YG1T, MG1T	VM15SC-1	100	0.5	E-0	3G1-3	1.5	20.0	1½	20	23
YG1K, YGS1, YGS1T	VM15SC-1	100	0.5	E-2	3G1-2	1.5	17.5	1¾	40	23
G5S	VM16SC	100	0.5	E-2	3G9-3	2.5	25.0	1¾	30	20.5
YG5T	VM16SC	120	0.5	E-2	3G9-4	2.5	25.0	1½	30	20.5
G6S	VM16SC	100	0.5	E-2	3G9-3	2.5	25.0	1¾	30	20.5
G6SB, G7S	VM16SC	120	0.5	E-2	3G9-3	2.5	25.0	1¾	30	22.5
HT1, HT1B	VM20SC	85	—	N-6	4D3-3	2.0	30.0	1¾	40	21
LT2	VM20SH	120	0.5	N-6	4J13-2	1.5	25.0	1¾	30	21
HS1, HS1B	VM16SC	70	—	E-0	3G9-4	1.5	20.0	1½	30	22.5
LS2	VM17SC	70	0.8	0-0	3D12-3	2.0	15.0	1¾	40	22.5
YL2, YL2C	VM17SC	120	2.0	D-0	3D3-3	2.0	20.0	1½	40	22
YL2CM	VM20SC	95	—	N-8	4D2-3	2.0	30.0	1¾	40	22
L5T, L5TA	VM20SC	180	2.0	O-8	4D2-3	2.0	20.0	1¾	40	22
YL1	VM16	60	—	E-0	3D3-3	1.5	17.5	2½	15	23
YL1E	VM16SC	60	2.0	E-0	3D3-3	1.5	17.5	2½	15	23
YA5	M21S1	120	—	—	22M3-3	—	30.0	1¾	—	—
YA6	VM22SC	190	2.0	O-0	4J6-3	2.5	30.0	1¾	110	25
AT1, AT1B, AT1C	VM24SH	150	—	N-8	4D3-3	2.0	30.0	1½	40	25.5
AT2	VM24SH	230	—	O-6	4F10-3	1.5	25.0	1¾	40	21
YAS1(c), AS2C	VM17SC	95	0.8	O-0	4D9-4	2.0	17.5	1¾	30	22
CT1, CT1B, CT1C	VM24SH	150	—	N-8	4D3-3	2.0	40.0	1½	40	25.5
CT2	VM24SH	200	—	O-6	4L6-3	2.0	25.0	2	40	21
YCS1	VM18SC	65	0.5	O-0	4D2-3	3.0	20.0	2	40	21
YCS1C, CS3C	VM20SC	65	—	N-6	4D10-3	2.5	30.0	2¼	40	21
CS3B, CS5	VM20SC	65	—	N-6	4D10-3	2.5	30.0	2	40	21.7
DT1	VM26SH	150	0.5	O-2	5D1-3	2.5	35.0	1½	60	14.1
DT1B, DT1S, D1 1C	VM26SH	160	0.8	O-2	5D1-3	2.5	35.0	1½	60	14.1
DT1E	VM26SH	160	—	O-2	5D1-3	2.5	35.0	1½	60	15.1
DS7	VM26SC	100	—	O-0	5DP7-4	2.0	40.0	1½	100	15.1
YDS2	VM20SH	80	—	N-6	24A1-3	2.0	25.0	1½	40	25
Early YDS3	VM24SC	120	0.5	O-0	4D4-2	2.0	20.0	1½	40	25
Early YDS3C	VM24SC	120	0.5	O-0	4D4-3	2.0	20.0	1½	40	25
Late YDS3, YDS3C	VM24	130	0.5	O-0	4D4-2	2.0	20.0	1½	40	25
YDS5	VM26SC	120	0.5	O-5	4D3-2	2.5	30.0	1½	40	25.5
DS6C	VM26SC	100	0.5	N-8	4D3-3	2.0	30.0	1½	40	25.5
DS6B	VM26SC	110	—	N-8	4D3-3	2.0	30.0	1½	40	25.5
DT2	VM26SH	160	—	N-8	5DP7-3	1.5	30.0	1¼	60	15.1
YM1	VM24	130	0.5	O-0	4D4-2	2.0	20.0	1½	40	25.1
YM2C	VM26SC	110	0.5	O-5	4D3-2	2.5	30.0	1½	40	25.5
YR1	VM28SC	190	0.5	O-2	5D1-2	1.5	30.0	2¼	40	25.5
YR2, YR2C, R3(C)	VM28SC	170	0.5	O-2	5D1-3	2.0	30.0	1½	40	25.5
R5, R5B	VM28SC	110	—	O-0	5DP7-4	2.0	40.0	1¾	100 ①	15
R5C	VM28SC	120	—	O-4	5DP7-4	2.0	30.0	1¼	100	15
RT1	VM32SH	240	—	O-4	6DP1-3	1.5	30.0	1¼	60	14.1
RT1B	VM32SH	240	—	O-4	6CF1-2	1.5	30.0	1¾	60	8.5
RT2	VM32SH	230	2.0	P-0	6DH3-3	3.0	45.0	1½	60	8.5

① Left carburetor only.   ② Measured in mm.

7 ● Electrical Systems

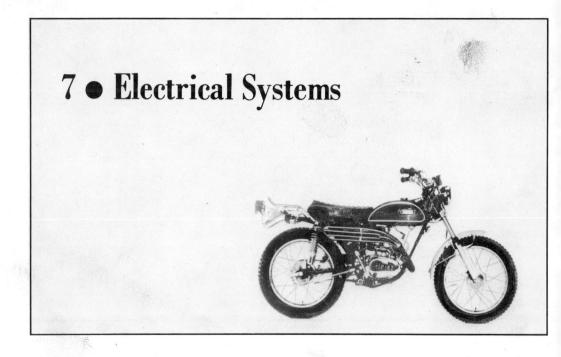

Yamaha motorcycles use four basic electrical systems: magneto, dc generator, starter generator, and alternator. A brief description of the operation of each type is given below.

Magneto

The magneto system uses ac current produced by a permanently magnetized flywheel, an ignition coil, and a lighting coil. The flywheel is secured to the end of the crankshaft and the coils are mounted in a fixed position within the flywheel circumference. The flywheel's rotating magnetic field cuts across the coil windings and, due to the constantly reversing magnetic field, induces an ac current through the coils.

The ignition coil current then travels through the condenser, points, secondary ignition coil (boosts the voltage), and spark plug. The light-ing coil current is connected to a load with the proper inductance, so that when current rises with engine rpm, resistance to the ac current increases. This serves to regulate voltage. The lighting coil is also connected to a silicon rectifier which converts the ac current to dc for charging the battery.

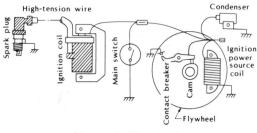

Magneto ignition circuit

DC Generator

The dc generator produces current in the same manner as an automobile generator. An armature made up of many looped wires around an iron core revolves within an electromagnet. The strong magnetic field of the magnet induces a voltage in the armature which is then picked up by carbon brushes that contact the commutator (where the looped armature wires meet). The current picked up by the brushes then passes through a voltage regulator

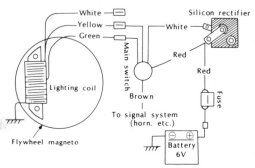

Magneto lighting circuit

110

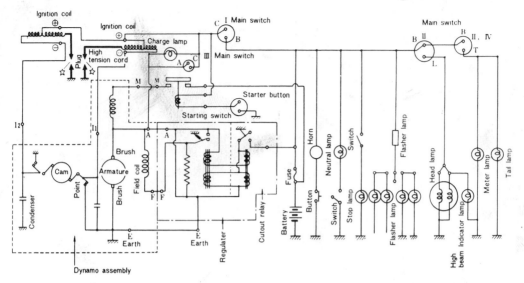

DC generator schematic

and to the condenser, points, ignition coil, spark plug, and lighting system.

ture (secured to the crankshaft), spins around and turns the engine.

Starter Generator

The starter generator operates similarly to the dc generator except that it has an additional electromagnet and an extra pair of brushes (older models). Current from the battery is sent to the windings of this electromagnet and to the armature via the carbon brushes. This current flow sets up a magnetic field in the armature and another surrounding the armature. The position of the north and south poles of these fields are contrasting, however, and since like poles repel and unlike poles attract, the arma-

Alternator

The alternator system produces ac current through a rotor and stator assembly. It operates in basically the same way as the magneto system, but in this case the permanent magnet (rotor) revolves within the fixed coils (stator or yoke). The current passes from the stator to a selenium rectifier where it is converted into dc and used for ignition and lighting. A voltage regulator is also used to maintain a constant voltage and control the alternator output.

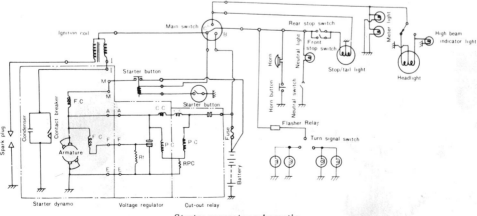

Starter generator schematic

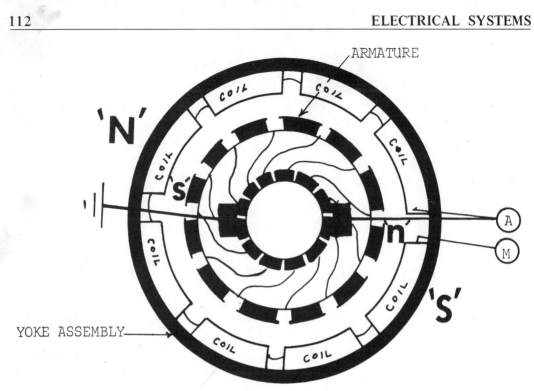

Starter generator electromagnetic fields

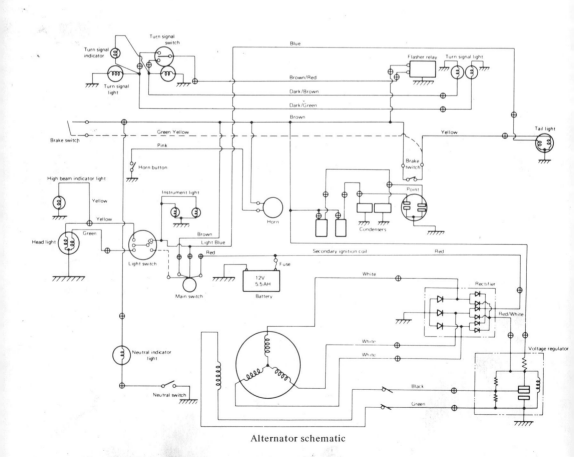

Alternator schematic

Component Tests

Use the following procedures in conjunction with the electrical specifications at the end of this chapter to determine faulty components.

DC Generator Voltage Output

1. Disconnect the generator wiring from the other components.

2. Connect a voltmeter to the armature terminal "A" (red) and ground field terminal "F" (black).

3. Run the engine up to about 2500 rpm and check the voltmeter reading. If within reasonable bounds of the necessary output (6 or 12 volts), the generator is not likely to be the source of your problem. If the output is nil or minimal, isolate the cause by checking the carbon brushes and field winding insulation.

   a. Check all brush wire connections.

   b. Measure brush length and spring tension.

   c. Make sure the positive carbon brush is properly insulated.

NOTE: Disconnect the negative brush before checking for a positive brush short.

Checking positive brush insulation

   d. Check for any dirt, oil, etc. that may be shorting out part of the yoke assembly.

   e. Check for proper continuity between the armature and field windings (terminals "A" and "F").

NOTE: Lift the carbon brushes off the commutator before checking field winding resistance.

   f. Check field winding insulation with an ohmmeter set at the highest scale. Readings between the yoke housing and terminal "A" and the yoke housing and terminal "F" should be infinite (3 megohms or more).

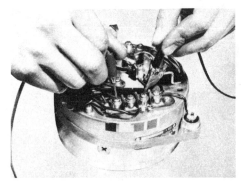

Checking continuity between the armature and field windings

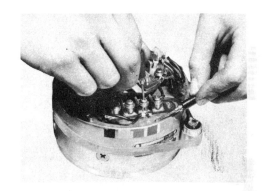

Checking field winding insulation

4. If the preceding tests didn't reveal the problem, perform the following checks on the armature:

   a. Make sure the mica gaps are free from any carbon dust that could short out the individual bars.

   b. Make sure the commutator surface is clean. If necessary, clean it up with a piece of fine emery cloth. Remember to remove the dust!

Cleaning up the commutator

   c. Check for continuity between the commutator segments and armature core. The readings should be infinite. There must be a completely open circuit!

Checking the commutator segments

d. Make sure continuity exists between all the commutator segments.

Starter Generator Brushes and Coil

1. Disconnect the negative starter brush and check the positive brush for insulation.

2. Disconnect the voltage regulator wiring and lift the positive brushes off the commutator. Make sure there is continuity between terminals "A" and "M". No resistance indicates a broken starter winding.

3. Disconnect the heavy motor winding wire from the positive brush and make sure the windings are insulated.

NOTE: On early models, the fields and motor windings are internally connected. The readings on these machines must be exactly as specified.

4. With the heavy motor winding wire still disconnected from the positive brush, make sure there is an open circuit between the "M" terminal and ground (at least 3 megohms).

Magneto Assembly

1. Make sure all connections are tight.
2. Check all parts for any oil or water spots.

3. The flywheel magnets eventually weaken. If the points and condenser are good, but lighting and spark are weak, replace the flywheel or have the magnets recharged.

4. Check the ignition and lighting coils for any signs of having burnt out.

5. Make sure the lighting coil wires all have continuity with each other.

6. Make sure there is no continuity between the ignition coil leads and core.

Alternator No Load Voltage Check

CAUTION: Never disconnect the battery from an ac generating system during operational tests.

1. Disconnect the yellow, green, and white wires from the stator.

2. Connect an ac voltmeter to the green and white wire leads, then start the engine. The voltage reading shows the output to the ignition system, battery, brake light, and horn.

3. Switch the ac voltmeter lead from the green wire to the yellow wire lead. This reading indicates output to the above mentioned components and also the lighting system.

Aternator Average Amperage Check

1. Disconnect the rectifier red wire.

2. Connect a dc ammeter positive lead to the red wire and connect the ammeter negative lead to the red wire connector.

3. Output at 3000 rpm should be 2.8 ± 0.5A—day position, 6.7 ± 0.5A—night position; at 5000 rpm, 3.2 ± 0.5A—day position and 7.1 ± 0.5A—night position.

Voltage Regulator Relay

NOTE: If isolating a problem source, first check the generator as previously described, then check this relay.

1. Check for any loose connections, broken solder, dirty points, etc.

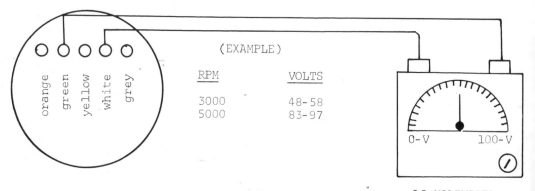

Checking alternator output to the daytime circuit

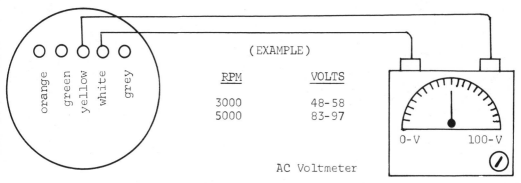

Checking alternator output to the nighttime circuit

2. Connect the correct voltage battery to the regulator coil as shown in the illustration, then insert a flat piece of steel into the electromagnetic field. If the steel is attracted by the field, the coil is OK.

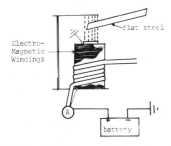

Checking the voltage regulator relay coil

3. Check the shunt resistors by connecting an ohmmeter positive lead to the "A" terminal and the negative lead to the "F" terminal. Manually operate the relay—each of the shunt positions should show a different resistance. If any of the positions indicate infinite resistance, one of the shunts is open.

4. Check the yoke, core, and point gap with specifications. Adjust if necessary.

5. Check the regulator no-load voltage by starting the engine, disconnecting the wire at

regulator terminal "B", connecting the positive lead of a voltmeter to the terminal and the negative lead to ground. Increase engine speed to the specified rpm and check the reading against specifications. The voltage can be adjusted by bending the spring hook or turning the adjusting screw so that the point pressure is increased or decreased.

NOTE: Increasing the pressure raises the voltage.

Voltage Cut-Out Relay

NOTE: Check the cut-out relay if the generator and voltage regulator relay are in good condition.

1. Check the relay magnetic field as previously described.

2. Check and adjust yoke, core, and point gap as previously described.

3. Check the relay cut-out voltage in the same manner as the regulator relay no-load voltage. If necessary, bend the point spring hook so that the cut-out voltage meets specifications.

Silicon Diode Rectifier (3-Wire) Continuity Check

1. Connect the positive lead of an ohmmeter to the red rectifier lead. Connect the negative lead to the green and then the white rectifier

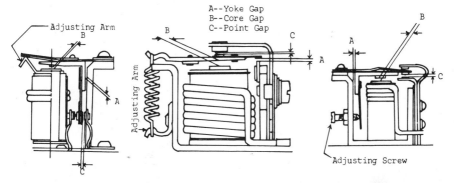

Voltage regulator relay adjustments

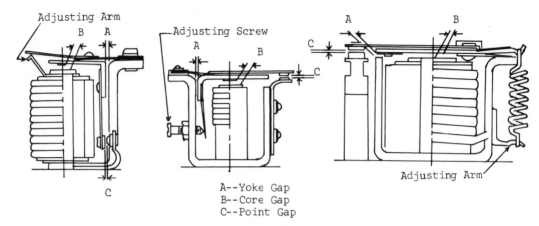

A--Yoke Gap
B--Core Gap
C--Point Gap

Cut-out relay adjustments

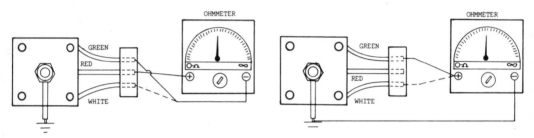

Schematic for checking silicon diode rectifiers

leads. The ohmmeter should show continuity. Reverse the meter leads and there should be no continuity.

2. Repeat the above with the ohmmeter connected to ground and the green, then the white rectifier leads.

Selenium Rectifier (2-Wire) Continuity Check

Connect an ohmmeter to the rectifier red and white wire leads, then reverse the meter leads. There should be continuity one way, but not the other.

Electric Starter Relay

If the starter motor does not function check the following:

1. Check for proper continuity in the starter relay core windings.

2. Check relay points for cleanliness.

3. When the points are closed, make sure there is continuity between the battery and motor windings.

NOTE: The starter relay is located either on the frame, as a separate unit, or within the voltage regulator housing.

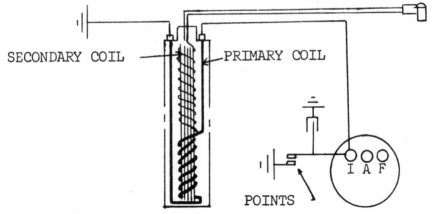

Ignition coil construction

Ignition Coil

NOTE: Check the ignition coil if you are having spark plug firing problems and the battery, points, and condenser checked out OK.

1. Check resistance between the positive and negative primary terminals.

2. Check continuity between one primary terminal and the high-tension secondary terminal. (should be around 6000 ohms).

3. Scrape some paint off the coil housing and check continuity between the primary winding and the coil housing. Resistance should read infinity.

4. Remove the plug cap and position the bare high-tension wire about 1/4 in. from the cylinder head. Kick the engine over and check for a strong bright spark.

CAUTION: Be very careful when handling the high-tension wire: it carries a lot of voltage and packs quite a wallop!

Electrical Wiring Color Codes

Chassis

Red—battery
Brown—current source wire
Dark Blue—lighting, switches
Green (in headlight shell)—low beam
Yellow (in headlight shell)—high beam
Pink—horn
Light Blue—neutral light
Yellow—stoplight switch
Green/Yellow—front stoplight switch
Blue/White—starter solenoid
Brown/White—turn signal switch
Dark Brown—left turn signal
Green—right turn signal

Magneto

Black—ignition (not ground)
Yellow—lighting
Green—daytime charging

Green/Red—nighttime charging
White—ignition switch to rectifier
White (from magneto)—no connection

Starter/Generator

Orange—ignition
Gray—ignition (twins)
Black—ground
Dark Green—fields
White—armature and charging light
Light Green—starter motor

Alternator

White (3)—AC output
Black—ground brush
Green—positive brush
Orange—ignition
Gray—ignition (twins

Electrical Specifications

DYNAMO & MAG	U5/U5L	U5E	YJ1/MJ2T/YJ2	JT1	YG1 (all)	YG5T	G5S
Type	Magneto	Starter Dyn.	Magneto	Magneto	Magneto	Starter Dyn.	Magneto
Contact Press. (kg)	0.83 ± 10%	0.5–0.7	0.83 ± 10%	0.60–0.80	0.7–0.9	0.70 ± 10%	0.70 ± 10%
Condenser Cap. (μf)	0.3 ± 10%	0.22 ± 10%	0.3 ± 10%	0.22 ± 10%	0.27 ± 10%	0.22 ± 10%	0.22 ± 10%
Stand. Brush Dimen. (mm)	—	5 x 8 x 20	—	—	—	4.5 x 8 x 20	—
Min. Brush Length (mm)	—	11.8	—	—	—	12.0	—
Brush Spring Strength (Kg)	—	0.40–0.56	—	—	—	0.6 ± 15%	—
Commutator Dia. (mm)	—	37.5	—	—	—	40.0	—
Commutator Wear Limit (mm)	—	2.0	—	—	—	2.0	—
Stand. Mica Undercut (mm)	—	0.5–1.0	—	—	—	0.5–1.0	—
Min. Mica Undercut (mm)	—	0.2	—	—	—	0.2	—
Field Coil Resist. (ohms)	—	5.0	—	—	—	6.1	—

CUT-OUT RELAY REGULATOR	U5/U5L	U5E U5E	U7E	YJ1/MJ2T/YJ2	JT1	JT2	YG1 (all)	YG5T	G55
Model No.	—	T10-6-52	T106-52A	—	—	—	—	RC2332W	
No Load Adj. (v @ rpm)	—	15.8–16.5 @ 2500	15.8–16.5 @ 2500	—	—	—	—	15.8–16.5 @ 2500	
Yoke Gap (mm)	—	0.6–0.7	0.6–0.7	—	—	—	—	—	—
Core Gap (mm)	—	0.4–0.7	0.4–0.5	—	—	—	—	1.1–1.2	—
Point Gap (mm)	—	0.4–0.5	11.8	—	—	—	—	0.3–0.4	—
Coil Resistance (ohms)	—	17.0	13.0	—	—	—	—	18.5	—
Cut-In Voltage	—	13 ± 0.5	0.2	—	—	—	—	13 ± 0.5	—
Yoke Gap (mm)	—	0.2	0.8–1.0	—	—	—	—	—	—
Core Gap (mm)	—	0.8–1.0	0.6–0.8	—	—	—	—	0.5–0.7	—
Point Gap (mm)	—	0.6–0.8	—	—	—	—	—	0.6–0.8	—

IGN. COIL	U5/U5L	U5E	U7E	YJ1/MJ2T/YJ2	JT1	JT2	YG1 (all)	YG5T	G55
Min. Spark Test (mm @ rpm)	6 @ 500	6 @ 100	8 @ 300	6 @ 500	7 @ 500	7 @ 500	6 @ 500	7 @ 500	7 @ 5
Sec. Wind. Resist. (ohms)	8K–9K	8K–9K	11K	8K–9K	11K	11K	4K	7K–8K	5K
Pri. Wind. Resist. (ohms)	4.5	4.5	4.0	4.9	4.9	4.9	—	0.6	0.6

STARTER RELAY	U5/U5L	U5E	U7E	YJ1/MJ2T/YJ2	JT1	JT2	YG1 (all)	YG5T	G55
Core Gap (mm)	—	1.4–1.5	1.3–1.4	—	—	—	—	1.2–1.4	—
Point Gap (mm)	—	1.3–1.4	1.4–1.5	—	—	—	—	1.3–1.5	—
Wind. Resist. (ohms)	—	4.6	—	—	—	—	—	11.2	—
Activating Volt. (min)	—	10	12	—	—	—	—	8	—

BATTERY	U5/U5L	U5E	U7E	YJ1/MJ2T/YJ2	JT1	JT2	YG1 (all)	YG5T	G55
Capacity	6V-7AH	12V-5.5AH	12V-7AH	6V-4AH	—		6V-2AH	6V-4AH	6V-4A

Electrical Specifications, continued

DYNAMO AND MAGNETO	G6S/G6SB/GS7	HT1/HT1B	LT2	HS1/HS1B	LS2	YL2	YL2C(m)/L5T(A)	YL1
Type	Magneto	Magneto	Magneto	Alternator	Magneto	Generator	Starter Dyn.	Generator
Contact Pressure (kg)	0.65–0.85	0.65–0.85	0.65–0.85	0.60–0.80	0.5–0.7	0.7 ± 10%	0.7 ± 10%	0.5–0.7
Condenser Capacity (μf)	0.22	0.25	0.30	0.22	0.22	0.22 ± 10%	0.22 ± 10%	0.22 ± 10%
Stand. Brush Dim. (mm)	—	—	—	—	—	4.5 x 8 x 20	4.5 x 8 x 20	4.5 x 8 x 20
Min. Brush Length (mm)	—	—	—	—	—	12.0	12.0	12.0
Brush Spring Strength (Kg)	—	—	—	—	—	0.6 ± 15%	0.6 ± 15%	0.6 ± 10%
Commutator Dia. (mm)	—	—	—	—	—	40.0	40.0	40.0
Com. Wear Limit (mm)	—	—	—	—	—	2.0	2.5	2.0
Stand. Mica Undercut (mm)	—	—	—	—	—	0.5–1.0	0.5–1.0	0.5–0.8
Min. Mica Undercut (mm)	—	—	—	—	—	0.2	0.2	0.2
Field Coil Resistance (ohms)	—	—	—	—	—	5.2	5.2	5.2
REGULATOR								
Model No.	—	—	—	—	—	RN226J2	RC2332W	T106-01
No Load Adj. (v @ rpm)	—	—	—	—	—	15.6–16.3 @ 2500	15.8–16.5 @ 2500	15.6–16.3 @ 2500
Yoke Gap (mm)	—	—	—	—	—	0.3	0.3	0.6–0.7
Core Gap (mm)	—	—	—	—	—	1.0–1.2	1.0–1.2	0.4–0.7
Point Gap (mm)	—	—	—	—	—	0.3–0.4	0.3–0.4	0.4–0.5
Coil Resistance (ohms)	—	—	—	—	—	18.5	18.5	17.0
CUT-OUT RELAY								
Cut-in Voltage	—	—	—	—	—	1.3 ± 0.5	1.3 ± 0.5	1.3 ± 0.5
Yoke Gap (mm)	—	—	—	—	—	0.3	0.3	0.2
Core Gap (mm)	—	—	—	—	—	0.5–0.7	0.5–0.7	0.8–1.0
Point Gap (mm)	—	—	—	—	—	0.6–0.8	0.6–0.8	0.6–0.8
IGN. COIL								
Min. Spark Test (mm @ rpm)	7 @ 500	7 @ 500	7 @ 500	7 @ 500	8 @ 300	6 @ 100	6 @ 100	6 @ 100
Sec. Wind. Resist. (ohms)	5.8K ± 10%	11K	6.6K	5K–8K	11K	7K–8K	7K–8K	5K–6K
Prim. Wind. Resist. (ohms)	0.6 ± 10%	4.9 ± 10%	1.6	4.2–5.2	4.0	4.8	4.8	4.7
STARTER RELAY								
Core Gap (mm)	—	—	—	—	—	—	1.2–1.4	—
Point Gap (mm)	—	—	—	—	—	—	1.3–1.5	—
Wind. Resistance (ohms)	—	—	—	—	—	—	11	—
Activating Voltage (min)	—	—	—	—	—	—	8	—
BATTERY								
Capacity	6V–4AH	6V–2AH	6V–4AH	12V–5.5AH	12V–5.5AH	12V–5.5AH	12V–7AH	12V–5.5AH

Electrical Specifications, continued

DYNAMO AND MAGNETO	YL1E	YA5	YA6	AT1/AT1B/ AT1C/AT2	YAS1(c)/ AS2C	CT1, CT1B, CT1C	CT2
Type	Starter Dyn.	Starter Dyn.	Starter Dyn.	Starter Dyn.	Alternator	Magneto	Magnet
Contact Pressure (Kg)	0.5–0.7	0.5–0.7	0.5–0.7	0.5–0.7	0.6 ± 10%	0.6–0.8 ± 10%	0.65–0.8
Condenser Capacity (μf)	0.22 ± 10%	0.22 ± 10%	0.22 ± 10%	0.22 ± 10%	0.22 ± 10%	0.22 ± 10%	0.30
Stand. Brush Dimen. (mm)	5 x 8 x 20	4.5 x 8 x 19.5	4.5 x 8 x 19.5	4.5 x 9 x 20.5	—	—	—
Min. Brush Length (mm)	11.5	8.0	11.5	9.0	—	—	—
Brush Spring Strength (Kg)	0.40–0.56	0.40–0.56	0.40–0.50	0.40–0.56	—	—	—
Commutator Dia. (mm)	37.5	37.5	37.5	38.5	—	—	—
Comttr. Wear Limit (mm)	2.0	2.0	2.0	2.0	—	—	—
Stand. Mica Undercut (mm)	0.5–1.0	0.5–0.8	0.5–0.8	0.5–0.8	—	—	—
Min. Mica Undercut (mm)	0.2	0.2	0.2	0.2	—	—	—
Field Coil Resistance (ohms)	5.2	6.8	6.8	4.8	—	—	—
REGULATOR							
Model No.	T106–53	T107–11 (13)	T167–52	T107–17	—	—	—
No Load Adj. (V @ rpm)	15.8–16.5 @ 3000	15.4–16.5 @ 3000	15.8–16.2 @ 3000	15.8–16.5 @ 2500	—	—	—
Yoke Gap (mm)	0.6–0.7	0.9–1.0	0.6–0.7	0.6–0.7	—	—	—
Core Gap (mm)	0.4–0.7	0.6–0.7	0.4–0.5	0.4–0.7	—	—	—
Point Gap (mm)	0.4–0.5	0.4–0.5	0.4–0.5	0.4–0.5	—	—	—
Coil Resistance (ohms)	17.0	9.85	14.4	11.2	—	—	—
CUT-OUT RELAY							
Cut-In Voltage	13 ± 0.5	13 ± 0.5	13 ± 0.5	13 ± 0.5	—	—	—
Yoke Gap (mm)	0.2	0.9–1.0	0.6–0.7	0.2	—	—	—
Core Gap (mm)	0.8–1.0	0.6–0.7	—	0.8–1.0	—	—	—
Point Gap (mm)	0.6–0.8	0.7–0.8	0.6–0.7	0.6–0.8	—	—	—
IGN. COIL							
Min. Spark Test (mm @ rpm)	6 @ 100	6 @ 100	6 @ 100	6 @ 100	7 @ 500	7 @ 500	7 @ 50
Sec. Wind. Resist. (ohms)	5K–6K	5K–6K	5.5K	11K ± 20%	6K–7K	11K ± 20%	6.6K
Pri. Wind. Resist. (ohms)	4.7	4.9	4.9	4.0 ± 10%	4.7	4.9	1.6
STARTER RELAY							
Core Gap (mm)	1.4–1.5	—	1.4–1.5	1.3–1.4	—	—	—
Point Gap (mm)	1.3–1.4	2.0	1.3–1.4	1.5	—	—	—
Wind. Resistance (ohms)	4.6	4.94	11.3	4.5 ± 15%	—	—	—
Activating Voltage (min)	10	8	8	10	—	—	—
BATTERY							
Capacity	12V–5.5AH	12V–10AH	12V–10AH	12V–7AH	12V–5.5AH	6V–2AH	6V–4A

Electrical Specifications, continued

DYNAMO AND MAGNETO	YCS1(C)	C53C/C53B	CS5	D17 (all)	DT2	YD3/YDT1	YDS1	YDS2
Type	Starter Dyn.	Starter Dyn.	Starter Dyn.	Magneto	Magneto	Starter Dyn.	Generator	Generator
Contact Pressure (Kg)	$0.7 \pm 10\%$	$0.7 \pm 10\%$	$0.7 \pm 10\%$	$0.6 \pm 10\%$	$0.7 \pm 10\%$	0.7–0.85	0.5–0.6	0.5–0.6
Condenser Capacity (μf)	$0.22 \pm 10\%$	$0.22 \pm 10\%$	0.22	$0.25 \pm 10\%$	0.25	$0.22 \pm 10\%$	$0.22 \pm 10\%$	$0.22 \pm 10\%$
Stand. Brush Dimen. (mm)	4.5 x 8 x 20	4.5 x 8 x 20	4.5 x 8 x 20	—	—	4.5 x 8 x 19.5	18 (length only)	18 (length only)
Min. Brush Length (mm)	12.0	12.0	8.0	—	—	8.0	12.0	12.0
Brush Spring Strength (Kg)	$0.6 \pm 15\%$	$0.6 \pm 15\%$	$0.6 \pm 15\%$	—	—	0.40–0.56	0.5–0.7	0.5–0.7
Commutator Dia. (mm)	40.0	40.0	40.0	—	—	37.5	35.0	35.0
Commtr. Wear Limit (mm)	2.0	2.0	2.0	—	—	2.0	1.0	1.0
Stand. Mica Undercut (mm)	0.5–1.0	0.5–1.0	0.5	—	—	0.5–0.8	0.5–0.8	0.5–0.8
Min. Mica Undercut (mm)	0.2	0.2	0.2	—	—	0.2	0.2	0.2
Field Coil Resistance (ohms)	5.0	4.9	4.9	—	—	9.04	4.06	4.06
REGULATOR								
Model No.	RC2333V	T107-S5	RC2333V	—	—	T107-03	RHG	RHG
Load Adj. (V @ rpm)	15.6–16.3 @ 2500	15.6–16.3 @ 2500	15.6–17.2 @ 4000	—	—	15.3–16.4 @ 3000	7.6–8.0 @ 3000	7.1–7.7 @ 3000
Core Gap (mm)	0.3	0.3	1.0–1.2	—	—	0.9–1.0	0.30–0.45	0.30–0.45
Wire Gap (mm)	1.0–1.2	1.0–1.2	—	—	—	0.6–0.7	0.9–1.1	0.9–1.1
Point Gap (mm)	0.3–0.4	0.3–0.4	0.3–0.4	—	—	0.4–0.5	—	—
Coil Resistance (ohms)	18.5	8.1 @ 20°C	8.1 @ 20°C	—	—	10.1	—	—
CUT-OUT RELAY								
Cut-In Voltage	13 ± 0.5	13 ± 0.5	14.0	—	—	13 ± 1.5	6.5–7.0	6.5–7.0
Core Gap (mm)	0.3	0.3	0.3–0.5	—	—	0.9–1.0	0.25 ± 0.15	0.25 ± 0.15
Wire Gap (mm)	0.3–0.5	0.3–0.5	—	—	—	0.6–0.7	0.4 ± 0.1	0.4 ± 0.1
Point Gap (mm)	0.7–0.9	0.7–0.9	0.7–0.9	—	—	0.7–0.8	0.4–0.6	0.4–0.6
IGN. COIL								
Max. Spark Test (mm @ rpm)	6 @ 100	7 @ 500	7 @ 1500	6 @ 500	7 @ 500	6 @ 100	6 @ 800	6 @ 500
Pri. Wind. Resist. (ohms)	7K–8K	7.2K	11K	5K–6K	6.5K	5.5K	5.5K	5.5K
Sec. Wind. Resist. (ohms)	4.8	4.8	4.0	0.6	0.9	4.9	1.7	1.7
STARTER RELAY								
Core Gap (mm)	1.2–1.4	1.2–1.4	1.3–1.5	—	—	—	—	—
Point Gap (mm)	1.3–1.5	1.3–1.5	1.2–1.4	—	—	2.0	—	—
Wind. Resistance (ohms)	11.2	11.2	11.2	—	—	4.94	—	—
Activating Voltage (min)	8	8	12	—	—	8	—	—
BATTERY								
Capacity	12V–9AH	12V–9AH	12V–9AH	6V–7AH	6V–4AH	N.A.	N.A.	N.A.

Electrical Specifications, continued

DYNAMO AND MAGNETO	YDS3(C)/ YM1	DS5	DS6C	DS6B	DS7	YM2(C)	YR1/YR2(C)/ R3(C)
Type	Generator	Starter Dyn.	Generator	Generator	Alternator	Generator	Generator
Contact Pressure (Kg)	$0.7 \pm 10\%$	$0.7 \pm 10\%$	$0.7 \pm 10\%$	$0.7 \pm 10\%$	$0.7 \pm 10\%$	$0.7 \pm 10\%$	$0.7 \pm 10\%$
Condenser Capacity (μf)	$0.22 \pm 10\%$	$0.22 \pm 10\%$	$0.22 \pm 10\%$	$0.22 \pm 10\%$	0.22	$0.22 \pm 10\%$	$0.22 \pm 10\%$
Stand. Brush Dimen. (mm)	5 x 9 x 17	4.5 x 8 x 20	4.5 x 8 x 20	4.5 x 8 x 20	6 x 7 x 11	4.5 x 8 x 20	4.5 x 8 x 20
Min. Brush Length (mm)	11.0	12.0	8.0	12.0	6.0	12.0	12.0
Brush Spring Strength (Kg)	$0.6 \pm 15\%$	$0.6 \pm 15\%$	0.6	0.6	0.62	0.6	0.6
Commutator Dia. (mm)	35.0	40.0	40.0	40.0	—	40.0	40.0
Cmttr. Wear Limit (mm)	1.0	2.0	2.0	2.0	—	2.0	2.0
Stand. Mica Undercut (mm)	0.5–1.0	0.5–1.0	0.5–1.0	0.5–1.0	—	0.5–1.0	0.5–1.0
Min. Mica Undercut (mm)	0.2	0.2	0.2	0.2	—	0.2	0.2
Field Coil Resist. (ohms)	4.2	5.0	5.57	5.6	4.2	5.6	5.6
REGULATOR							
Model No.	RN6225K	RN2225M	RN2226J	RN2226J	RL215	RN2226J	RN2226J ①
No Load Adj. (V @ rpm)	7.7–8.1 @ 2500	15.6–16.3 @ 2500	15.6–16.3 @ 2500	15.6–16.3 @ 2500	14.0–15.5 @ 4000	15.6–16.3 @ 2500	15.6–16.3 @ 2500
Yoke Gap (mm)	0.3	—	—	—	0.7–1.2	—	—
Core Gap (mm)	1.1–1.4	1.0–1.2	1.0–1.2	1.0–1.2	0.8–1.1	1.0–1.2	1.0–1.2
Point Gap (mm)	0.3–0.4	0.3–0.4	0.3–0.4	0.3–0.4	0.3–0.4	0.3–0.4	0.3–0.4
Coil Resistance (ohms)	5.6	18.5	18.5	18.5	10.8	18.5	18.5
CUT-OUT RELAY							
Cut-in Voltage	6.5–7.0	13 ± 0.5	13 ± 0.5	13 ± 0.5	—	13 ± 0.5	13 ± 0.5
Yoke Gap (mm)	0.3	—	—	—	—	—	—
Core Gap (mm)	0.3–0.5	0.3–0.5	0.3–0.5	0.3–0.5	—	0.3–0.5	0.3–0.5
Point Gap (mm)	0.7–0.9	0.7–0.9	0.7–0.9	0.7–0.9	—	0.7–0.9	0.7–0.9
IGN. COIL							
Min. Sprk. Test (mm @ rpm)	6 @ 100	6 @ 100	7 @ 100	7 @ 700	7 @ 500	6 @ 100	6 @ 100
Sec. Wind. Resist. (ohms)	5K–6K	7K–8K	8.2K	8.2K	11K	7K–8K	7K–8K
Pri. Wind. Resist. (ohms)	1.6	4.8	4.6	4.6	4.0	4.8	4.8
STARTER RELAY							
Core Gap (mm)	—	1.1–1.3	—	—	—	—	—
Point Gap (mm)	—	2.05–2.35	—	—	—	—	—
Wind. Resistance (ohms)	—	4.3	—	—	—	—	—
Activating Voltage (min)	—	8	—	—	—	—	—
BATTERY							
Capacity	6V–7AH	12V–11AH	12V–5AH	12V–5AH	12V–5.5AH	12V–5.5AH	12V–5.5AH

① R3—R2220J

Electrical Specifications, continued

DYNAMO AND MAGNETO	R5/R5B	R5C	RT1–RT1B	RT2	XS1/XS1B	XS2
Type	Alternator	Alternator	Magneto	Magneto	Alternator	Alternator
Contact Pressure (Kg)	0.6–0.8	0.65–0.75	0.6 ± 10%	0.6–0.8	0.75	0.56–0.65
Condenser Capacity (μf)	0.22	0.22	0.25 ± 10%	0.25	0.22	0.22
Stand. Brush Dimensions (mm)	11.5 x 7 x 6	—	—	6 x 7 x 11	14.5 (length only)	4.5 x 4.5 x 14.5
Min. Brush Length (mm)	6.0	—	—	6.0	7.0	7.5
Brush Spring Strength (Kg)	—	—	—	0.62	—	0.8
Commutator Dia. (mm)	—	—	—	—	—	—
Commutator Wear Limit (mm)	—	—	—	—	—	—
Stand. Mica Undercut (mm)	—	—	—	—	—	—
Min. Mica Undercut (mm)	—	—	—	—	—	—
Field Coil Resistance (ohms)	—	—	—	4.2–4.3	0.6②	5.15
REGULATOR						
Model No.	—	—	—	RL2150X	TLIZ-40	TLIX-49
No Load Adj. (V @ rpm)	15.5–16.5 @	—	—	14.0–15.5 @ 4000	19.5 ± 0.5 @ 2000	14.5 @ 1500
Yoke Gap (mm)	—	—	—	0.7–1.2	0.9	—
Core Gap (mm)	—	—	—	0.8–1.1	0.6–1.0	—
Point Gap (mm)	—	—	—	0.3–0.4	0.3–0.4	—
Coil Resistance (ohms)	—	—	—	10.8	—	—
CUT-OUT RELAY						
Cut-In Voltage	—	—	—	—	—	14
Yoke Gap (mm)	—	—	—	—	—	—
Core Gap (mm)	—	—	—	—	—	—
Point Gap (mm)	—	—	—	—	—	—
IGN. COIL						
Min. Spark Test (mm @ rpm)	8 @ 500	7 @ 500	6 @ 500	7 @ 500	8 @ 300	7 @ 500
Secondary Wind. Resistance (ohms)	11K	6.5K	5K–6K	11K	11K ± 10%	11K
Primary Wind. Resistance (ohms)	5.0	0.9	0.6	4.0	3.9 ± 10%	4.0
STARTER RELAY						
Core Gap (mm)	—	—	—	—	—	1.5–1.88
Point Gap (mm)	—	—	—	—	—	0.88–1.11
Wind. Resistance (ohms)	—	—	—	—	—	8.5
Activating Voltage (min)	—	—	—	—	—	6.5
BATTERY						
Capacity	12V–5.5AH	6V–4AH	6V–2AH	12V–5.5AH	12V–5.5AH	12V–12AH

Between any two white wires.   ③ 13°–17° (ret.); 40° (adv.).   ④ 13°–17° (ret); 42° (adv.).

8 ● Chassis

This chapter deals with the wheels, frame, suspension, and associated parts. An important point to keep in mind when removing or installing these components is that they are all subject to a great deal of vibration. Make sure the spokes, axles and securing bolts are well tightened and that all cotter pins are correctly installed.

Front Wheel

Removal

1. Disconnect the brake cable, first from the handle bar, then from the wheel hub.
2. Disconnect the speedometer drive cable from the wheel hub.
3. Remove the securing cotter pin, then the axle nut.

Disconnecting the brake cable at the front wheel

Removing the front axle nut

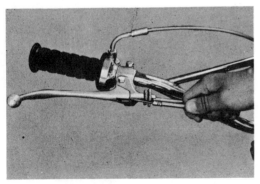

Disconnecting the brake cable at the handlebars

4. Loosen the axle locknuts or bolts.
5. Block up the bike under the engine, then pull out the axle and remove the wheel assembly.

Removing the front axle securing bolts

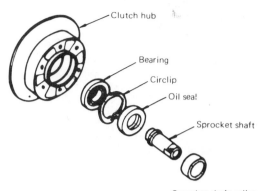

Front hub assembly

Inspection and Assembly

1. Anchor the wheel assembly as shown in the illustration and measure wheel rim runout. The maximum deviation is 2.0 mm (0.07 in.).

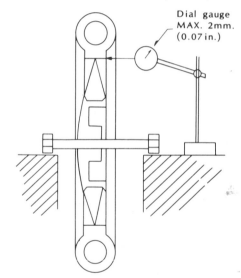

Measuring rim runout

Removing the front axle

2. Make sure all the spokes are tight. If possible, tighten each nipple to 15 kg/cm (13 in. lbs).

Removing the front wheel

Hub Disassembly

1. Push out the sprocket shaft.
2. Remove the sprocket shaft collar.
3. Remove the clutch hub bearing oil seal and retaining circlip.
4. Push out the clutch hub bearing.
5. Using the bent end of the special tool and a hammer, drive out the wheel bearing spacer.
6. Remove the wheel bearing.

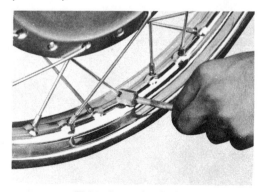

Tightening spoke nipples

3. Check the brake shoes for excessive wear and replace them if necessary. If the linings are glazed, rough them up with sandpaper; if they are oil soaked, replace them.

Cleaning up a glazed brake shoe

4. Check the axle for straightness and replace it if necessary.

5. Inspect the speedometer drive gear for burrs, etc., and replace it if excessively worn.

6. Check the bearings for scoring, pitting, or looseness in their races.

7. Pack the bearings in grease, then reassemble the wheel with new oil seals.

8. Install the wheel in the reverse of removal, using a new axle nut cotter pin.

Rear Wheel

Removal

1. Disconnect the rear brake rod or cable.
2. Disconnect the brake plate torque arm.

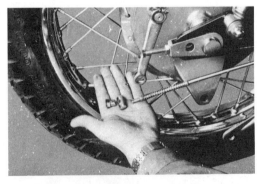

Disconnecting the rear brake rod

3. Loosen the chain adjusters on both sides.
4. Remove the retaining cotter pin, then remove the axle nut.

Disconnecting the rear brake torque arm

Loosening the chain adjustors

Removing the rear axle nut

5. Pull out the axle.

Tapping out the rear axle

6. Remove the right chain adjuster and distance collar.

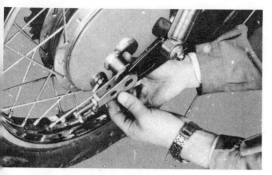

Removing the right chain adjustor

7. Slip the chain off the rear sprocket.

8. Remove the brake backing plate and roll out the wheel assembly.

Disassembly and Assembly

1. If the sprocket and hub remain on the bike, remove the sprocket shaft nut, axle, and sprocket assembly.

2. Bend back the locking tabs and remove the sprocket holding bolts.

3. Inspect bearings, etc., as described for the front wheel and measure the rim for runout.

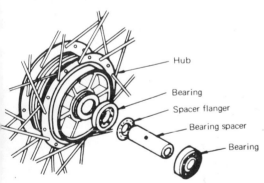

Rear wheel hub assembly

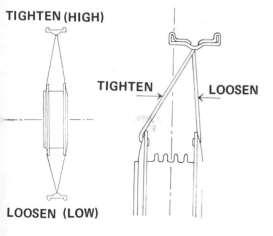

4. Reverse the disassembly and removal procedures for assembly and installation.

Front Fork (Enduro Type)

Removal and Disassembly

1. Remove the front wheel.
2. Remove the front fender.
3. Remove the fork leg caps.
NOTE: It may be necessary to loosen and pivot the handlebars for clearance.
4. Loosen the steering head bracket bolts.

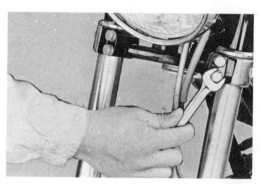

Loosening the steering head pinch bolts

5. Pull out the fork legs.

6. Remove the fork springs and drain the inner tubes.

7. Remove the Allen bolt at the bottom of each leg, then separate the inner and outer tubes.

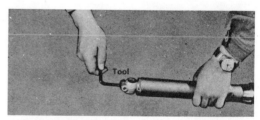

Removing the inner/outer leg securing allen bolt

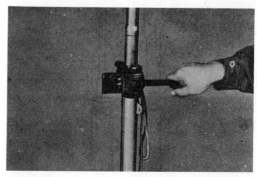

Separating inner and outer tubes with a strap wrench

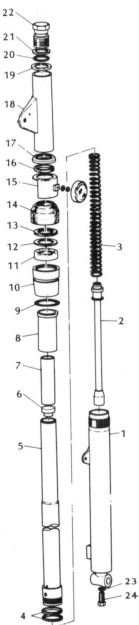

1 Outer tube
2 Cylinder complete
3 Fork spring
4 Piston ring
5 Inner tube
6 Spring upper seat
7 Spacer
8 Slide metal
9 O-ring
10 Outer nut
11 Oil seal
12 Oil seal washer

13 Oil seal clip
14 Dust seal
15 Outer cover
16 Packing (lamp stay)
17 Cover under guide
18 Upper cover
19 Cover upper guide
20 Packing (O-ring)
21 Cap washer
22 Cap bolt
23 Packing
24 Bolt

Typical Enduro fork leg construction

Assembly and Installation

1. Replace the inner tube oil seal.

2. Assemble each leg in the reverse order of disassembly.

3. Pull each fork leg through the steering head and hold it in the uppermost position with the special holding tool, then tighten the steering head bracket bolts.

4. Fill the inner tubes with the proper amount of oil, then reinstall the fork caps.

Front Fork
(Standard Telescopic Type)

Removal and Disassembly

1. Remove the front wheel and fender.
2. Remove the fork leg caps.
3. Loosen the underbracket bolts.
4. Pull out the inner tubes and drain the oil.

Separating standard fork inner and outer tubes

5. Protect the outer tube nut with a piece of rubber, then clamp it in a vise.

6. Using the front axle as a lever, twist the inner tube counterclockwise and separate it from the outer tube.

7. Replace the oil seals, check the inner tube for straightness, then assemble in the reverse of

Installing the front fork legs with the special holding tool

the removal procedure and install as described for the Enduro type fork.

Rear Shock Absorbers

Test the rear shocks by compressing them against the floor, then releasing them. If the shock expands quickly half way, then slowly the remaining distance, it is OK. If it expands quickly the entire distance, the oil has leaked out and the shock should be replaced.

Testing the rear shock absorber

Rear Swing Arm

Before removing the swing arm, check it for excessive wear. Do this by moving it back and forth laterally: if there is evidence of play, either the swing arm bushing or shaft must be replaced.

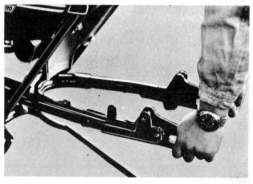

Checking rear swing arm lateral freeplay

To remove the swing arm:
1. Remove the chain guard.
2. Remove the swing arm shaft nut.
3. Pull out the shaft and lift off the arm.
4. Reverse the above for installation.

9 ● Performance and Racing Modifications

Before planning the metamorphosis of your Yamaha, carefully consider the following points:

1. Responsibility for any modifications whatsoever falls ENTIRELY on the owner. Yamaha International Corporation honors no warranty claims due to any associated parts or alterations, and makes no specific recommendations relating to performance modification. GYT parts and racing specifications are provided purely as a customer service, and the factory cannot be held liable for any resultant effects or damages.

2. A gain in one aspect of performance ALWAYS sacrifices another.

3. In order to achieve a noticeable power increase, engine performance modifications must be treated as a whole. In most cases, replacing or altering one component within a system will have a negligible effect on total output.

4. Engine life and reliability will decrease proportionately to the extent of modifications.

5. Any in-depth performance work requires a considerable investment of time, money and patience.

If the desire to modify your Yamaha still remains unshaken, approach your plans realistically, and determine whether or not what you want is feasible. It would be very foolish, for example, to try turning a YR1 into a scrambles machine. By the time your modifications made it even halfway competent in the rough, you would have spent enough time, energy, and money to have bought and put 5000 miles on an Enduro model. The Enduro machine would still be the better performer in the dirt!

Every motorcycle has its design limitations. Keep them in mind and don't attempt to turn your bike into something it isn't capable of being.

Improving Standard Performance

There are several changes that can be made to improve overall performance without making the machine illegal for street use. Actually, many of these changes could be called personalization because they deal mainly with modifications to suit the owner and the type of riding he does.

Gearing

Manufacturers usually select a machine's final drive ratio so that the engine can almost (but not quite) reach redline in top gear with an average rider abroad. Since many riders don't fit into the average category, this doesn't always work out. In most of these cases, the engine is unable to reach peak power in top gear, resulting in both poor acceleration and a low top speed.

A noticeable improvement can often be achieved by changing the final drive ratio (no. of rear-wheel sprocket teeth/no. of countershaft sprocket teeth). A suitable new ratio will usually improve not only acceleration, but top speed as well, because the engine will reach peak rpm in top gear. To change the ratio, you can choose either a larger rear-wheel sprocket or a smaller countershaft sprocket. Changing the rear sprocket allows a wider choice of ratios; changing the countershaft sprocket is easier and less expensive.

In order to select an appropriate replacement, determine what effect different sprockets will have on engine and road speeds. To calculate the THEORETICAL top speed of any motorcycle in any given gear:

1. Determine the rear tire diameter by making a chalk line on the tire and measuring the distance it travels (in feet) during one complete revolution. Divide this distance into 5280 feet for the number of tire revolutions per mile. A 4.00 X 18 tire will turn approximately 785 times, a 3.50 X 18 approximately 815 times, a 3.00 X 18 approximately 840 times, and a 2.50 X 17 approximately 890 times.

2. Calculate the OVERALL gear ratio by using the following formula:

$$\frac{\text{no. clutch gear teeth} \times \text{no. rear sprocket teeth}}{\text{no. primary gear teeth} \times \text{no. countershaft sprocket teeth}} = \text{Overall Gear Ratio}$$

Then, multiply the overall gear ratio by the transmission ratio for the chosen gear (see General Specifications). For example, an overall gear ratio of 5.1 multiplied by a 5th-gear transmission ratio of 0.9 equals an overall 5th-gear ratio of 4.59.

3. Using the engine's peak rpm and the products of Steps 1 and 2, determine the computed top speed:

$$\text{Top Speed} = \frac{(60) \times (\text{engine peak rpm})}{\left(\text{tire r/p/mile}\right) \times \left(\text{overall ratio for given gear}\right)}$$

In actual application, the computed top speeds are rarely achieved due to several limiting factors: engine output, vehicle weight, tire expansion, wind resistance, etc. The figures will, however, provide a reference from which to work, and when combined with known characteristics of a certain machine, can give an accurate estimation of engine rpm and corresponding road speeds.

Wheels and Tires

TIRE TREAD PATTERNS

Many different tread types are available to suit various conditions; evaluate the kind of ter-rain you usually ride on, then select the most appropriate tread. In general, universal dirt- or trials-type tires provide the best traction on medium- and hard-packed surfaces; knobby-type tires give the most bite in mud or soft sand.

On street machines, the standard ribbed or patterned front, and universal rear tires give the best overall performance and mileage. If you enjoy a lot of high-speed cornering, any of the new cling compound tires will stick to the pavement a little better, although the extra traction will somewhat sacrifice tire life.

OVERSIZE TIRES AND RIMS

At one time or another, most aspiring street and off-road riders get the bug to mount oversized tires. Larger tires give most motorcycles a leaner, more aggressive appearance, even though they seldom offer any advantages.

Unfortunately, many riders simply make the modification without first considering the overall effect of larger tires on the machine's handling characteristics. Here are four important points to keep in mind when making any changes:

STEERING GEOMETRY—In order to maintain the correct trail angle and distance relationship, equal tire and/or wheel size changes must be made front and rear. For example, if a 2.75 X 18 front and a 3.00 X 18 rear is standard, you can switch (theoretically) to a 3.25 X 18 and 3.50 X 18, or a 2.75 X 19 and 3.50 X 18.

If you fail to make EQUAL changes, however, the machine's handling characteristics will radically change—usually for the worse.

NOTE: The most common tire sizes are 2.25, 2.50, 2.75, 3.00, 3.25, 3.50, 4.00, and 4.50 (Motocross racing tire).

RIM WIDTH AND DIAMETER—Motorcycle rim widths are most often designated WM-0, WM-1, WM-2, and WM-3. They can accept maximum tire sizes of 2.50, 3.00, 3.50, and 4.50, respectively. Make sure that the oversize tire and rim width are compatible, otherwise the bike will react slowly and feel very vague when negotiating a corner.

Readily available rim diameters in inches are 17, 18, 19, and 21. The only rim change that has proven practical on Yamahas is mounting a 21 in. front rim on Enduro models, 125cc or over, that are used almost exclusively in the woods. In most other cases, the standard diameter rims are the best.

TIRE FIT—Make sure that the oversized tires have sufficient clearance with the front forks and the rear shocks completely bottomed (fully compressed). If you ride the bike with too tight a fit, you may find yourself sprawled on the ground with a terrible headache.

GEARING AND SPEEDOMETER ERROR— Oversized tires will require a compensating final drive ratio change. A 0.25 in. increase in tire size should be accompanied by a one- or two-tooth increase in rear sprocket size in order to maintain approximately the original ratio.

Until recently, it has been very difficult to correct speedometer error caused by oversized wheels and tires. Several manufacturers, however, now offer a small unit that contains the appropriate reduction gears and fits under the speedometer housing. These units are available for most Yamahas equipped with any combination of the common wheel-and-tire sizes.

SECURITY BOLTS

If your wheels aren't already equipped with security bolts, it's a good idea to install them. These bolts hold the tire tightly against the rim and prevent it from slipping during hard braking and acceleration. On off-road machines, the bolts offer an extra advantage in that the rear tire pressure can be lowered for additional traction, without fear of tearing off the valve stem.

Suspension

FRONT FORK

You can adjust the front fork damping qualities to a limited degree by changing the viscosity of the fork oil. In most cases, a thicker oil is more desirable because it stiffens the fork action, and although small bumps become more noticeable, high-speed stability and handling will be greatly improved.

Of special interest to the off-road rider is beefier front fork springs. Replacement units for Enduro models are available from Yamaha dealers and several accessory manufacturers; stiffer springs to fit earlier machines can often be found on older Yamaha trail bikes.

Increased fork travel is another prime consideration for the off-road machine, but this usually involves replacing the entire fork assembly, and that can be rather expensive. For the rider who wants the extra travel, however, and doesn't mind the expense, there are many fine units available. Full-size Enduro owners can extend fork travel and have a generally stronger front end by installing the next larger assembly: the HT1 accepts the AT1/CT1 fork, the AT1/CT1 accept the DT1/RT1 units, and the interchanges can be made without modification.

REAR SHOCK ABSORBERS

The standard Yamaha adjustable shock absorbers are sufficient under most riding conditions—providing they are set at the appropriate spring tension position. For high-performance road handling, the stiff settings usually provide the best stability and control during hard braking and cornering, even though they give the machine a very firm ride.

If you want greater shock travel or heavier damping for off-road riding and decide to buy replacement shocks, it is advisable to get the rebuildable type. In addition to the virtue of replaceable parts, these units can be filled with various viscosity oils to achieve different damping characteristics. Owners of full-size Enduro models also have the option of installing shocks from any of the other bikes in the Enduro line. Here is a chart showing the various models and the units they use:

Model	Spring Rate (lb/ft/sec)	Damper Return Rate
AT1, AT1B, CT1B	60.5	87.1
DT1	77.3	57.5
CT1, DT1B, DT1C, RT1	77.3	87.1
AT1C, CT1C, DT1E, RT1B	N.A.	87.1

Weight Reduction

The gross weight of a motorcycle AND rider has as much bearing on the machine's performance as the engine's power output. The word "and" is emphasized because many riders tend to concentrate on the former while ignoring the latter—the rider's own weight.

As far as the motorcycle itself is concerned, weight reduction can be accomplished in several ways. Some owners, for example, remove the passenger foot-pegs, tool kit, centerstand, and other nonessential items. Trimming overall weight in this manner, however, usually results in more inconvenience than improvement in performance.

The first target of weight reduction should be unsprung components. These include any parts that are suspended from the bottom fork legs and rear shock absorbers: wheels, hubs, tires, rear swing arm, front fender, etc. When riding over rough roads, these unsprung components must rise and fall with the surface irregularities. If they are heavy, the movement is slow and the tires are unable to follow the irregularities accurately; if they are light, the movement is quick and the tires can follow each bump closely. Therefore, less unsprung weight spells better handling, as well as overall weight reduction.

The least expensive method of reducing unsprung weight is replacing the standard steel rims with their alloy counterparts. Alloy sprockets and alloy or fiberglass front fenders are also inexpensive, but the weight saving is less significant. A great deal of weight can also be reduced by replacing the hubs and swing arm, but the cost of super lightweight components can be astronomical and, therefore, not very practical.

Engine (Two-Stroke)

Once again, keep in mind the disadvantages of modifying your engine. You can only make it perform better at one particular rpm range, and the power everywhere else will be drastically reduced.

The main problem in modifying a street engine is that the biggest power improver for the two-stroke engine is tuned expansion chambers, which are illegal for street riding. Because of this, it is not recommended to use GYT parts, as they must be balanced by a tuned exhaust in order to perform effectively. A good rule of thumb to follow when modifying a street engine is to perform no more than 50% of the full race treatment for a particular machine. General information is given below.

INTAKE PORT

On a rotary-valve models grind out the valve opening and increase the valve cutaway by 5°-8°. Do not exceed 10° in any case.

On piston port engines, remove 2-3 mm (0.08-0.12 in.) from the bottom of the port. This will allow the port to open sooner and take more fuel into the combustion chamber.

When modifying any engine, always match the carburetor bore to the intake port. If necessary, grind the passage smooth.

EXHAUST PORT

The exhaust port should be exposed a little sooner, so remove 2-3 mm (0.08-0.12 in.) from the top of the port.

COMBUSTION CHAMBER

Remove 1.0-1.15 mm (0.04-0.045 in.) from the bottom of the cylinder head and reshape the bottom edge to the original configuration. Any modification beyond this will create overheating problems.

IGNITION

Leave the ignition system as is. Depending on the fuel used, you may advance the timing about 0.1 mm, but no more. Check the spark plug readings after all the modifications have been performed. If all goes well, you should need a one-step colder plug.

AIR CLEANER AND EXHAUST SYSTEM

Don't attempt to alter these components. With the above modifications, the standard air cleaner and muffler will suffice. Pay much more attention to the maintenance of these items because their cleanliness is very critical when the engine has been modified.

Engine (XS1/XS2)

Since the XS1/XS2 powerplant is relatively new to the Yamaha family, factory information for modifications is not available. Much research is currently being done by both the factory and privateers, but their emphasis is mainly on racing.

Yamaha dealers do carry one item that can noticeably improve the XS1/XS2 rpm range: competition valve springs. These heavy duty springs promote more positive closing of the valves and add about 900 rpm to the engine's rev limit.

Racing Modifications

Specific modification procedures are given below for those Yamahas that have proven the most suitable and popular for racing. Most of the earlier machines are no longer competitive as compared to today's out-of-the-crate road and dirt racers. They can, however, provide the novice rider with an inexpensive mount, or the backyard mechanic with an ideal project.

Use Yamaha GYT parts whenever possible. Kits containing all the necessary components are available for many recent machines, but are hard to find for older models. If you are forced to use modified stock components, bear in mind that they are not designed to withstand the additional stress of racing and are more likely to fail than their GYT counterparts.

Before making any replacements or modifications, the entire engine should be completely disassembled and all the parts measured for proper clearances, wear limits and general condition. When reassembling the engine, replace all the seals and gaskets, install the GYT or modified parts, and remember to tighten every nut and bolt to the specified torque. BE METICULOUS—a well prepared bike is as essential to winning races as the ability of the rider.

YJ1 (For Off-Road Racing)
CYLINDER HEAD

Use the GYT cylinder head or perform the following modifications on the stock head:

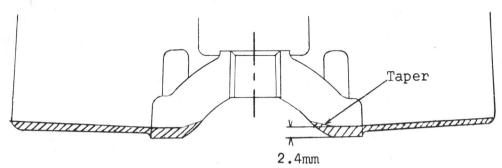

Taper

2.4mm

Modified YJ1 cylinder head

1. Machine 2.4 mm off the bottom of the head.

2. Remove approximately 1.5 mm along the bottom edge of the cooling fins.

3. Taper the bottom edge of the combustion chamber approximately 20°.

CYLINDER

Use the GYT cylinder or perform the following modifications on the stock cylinder:

1. Remove 2.5 mm from the top of the transfer ports.

2. Remove 2.0 mm from the top of the exhaust port.

3. Bevel the reshaped ports to eliminate any rough edges.

4. Reshape the exhaust port passage as shown in the illustration.

PISTON AND RINGS

Use the GYT piston or modify the stock piston by cutting a 5.0 mm × 20.0 mm notch in the piston skirt directly opposite the exhaust port (facing the transfer port).

If the piston is to be installed in the GYT cylinder, use two standard lower rings; in a modified cylinder, use both standard upper and lower rings.

NOTE: The stock upper ring and GYT cylinder cannot be used together because they are both chrome-plated and will not seat properly.

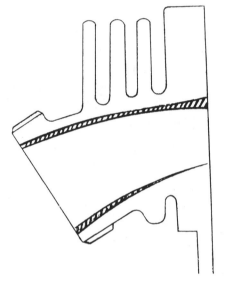

Modified YJ1 exhaust port

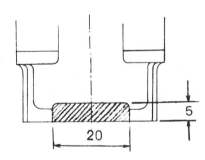

5

20

Modified YJ1 piston

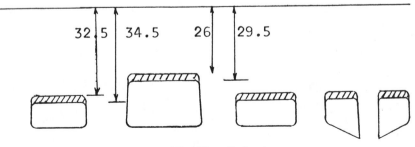

32.5   34.5   26   29.5

Modified YJ1 cylinder

PISTON FIT

Piston-to-cylinder wall clearance should be 0.040–0.050 mm with the GYT cylinder and 0.050–0.060 mm with the modified stock cylinder.

CARBURETOR

Replace the stock Mikuni VM14SC with the larger VM18SC (standard on the YCS1).

ROTARY VALVE

Use the GYT rotary valve or modify the stock valve by increasing the cutaway to 157° 30' (see illustration).

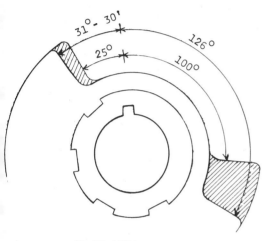

Modified YJ1 rotary valve

ROTARY-VALVE COVER

Use the GYT valve cover or perform the following modifications on the stock cover:
1. Enlarge the cover opening by removing the shaded area indicated in the illustration.
2. Make a cylindrical sleeve 14 mm wide with an inside diameter of approximately 20.0 mm,

then sand the inside surface until it fits snugly over the end of the cover.

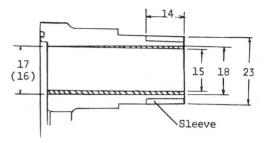

Modified YJ1 rotary-valve cover with sleeve

CRANKCASE INTAKE PORT

Enlarge the intake port as shown in the illustration and taper the bottom edge 7°. Mount the GYT or modified rotary valve, valve cover, and carburetor on the crankcase. Then check the alignment of the entire intake passage. All mating seams should be free of any steps or rough edges.

CRANKCASE COVER

Use the GYT cover to modify the stock cover by removing the shaded areas indicated in the illustration. This is necessary to give the larger carburetor sufficient clearance.

CARBURETOR COVER

Use the GYT carburetor cover if the GYT crankcase cover is used. If a modified stock crankcase cover is used, remove 7.0 mm from the carburetor air horn and install the stock carburetor cover.

NOTE: The YJ1 uses the same GYT carburetor cover as the YG1.

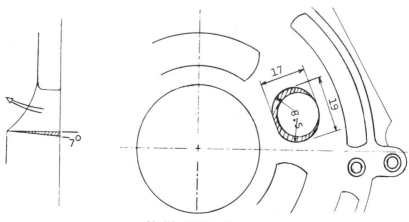

Modified YJ1 intake port

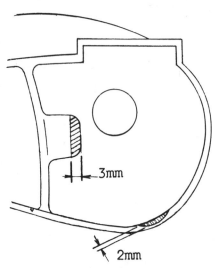

Modified YJ1 crankcase cover

the damping by filling the fork legs with 30 to 50W oil. Also modify the fork stops as shown in the illustration.

Use the GYT rear shock absorbers or stiffer units from a larger model. If necessary for rear sprocket clearance, modify the shock mounting points as shown in the illustration.

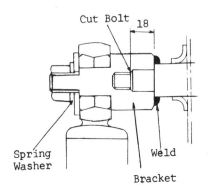

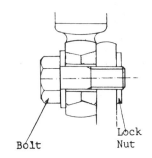

Modified YJ1 rear shock mount

CARBURETOR CAP

If GYT crankcase and carburetor covers are used, the GYT carburetor cap and cap plate must be installed. If modified stock covers are used, the stock cap can be used.

EXHAUST SYSTEM

Use the GYT expansion chamber assembly or have one made to the same dimensions. An expansion chamber MUST be used: it is the most critical single factor in two-stroke speed tuning.

ELECTRICAL SYSTEM

Use the stock magneto, but remove the lighting coil and all unnecessary accessories, lights, and wiring.

SUSPENSION

Use the front fork and brake backing plate from a YG1. Increase the spring rate by installing YG1, GYT, or YG1T springs and increase

TUNING SPECIFICATIONS

Ignition and fuel mixture settings vary greatly with atmospheric conditions, air temperature, and the type of racing to be done. The following is intended as a guide only and should be modified as necessary according to spark plug readings.

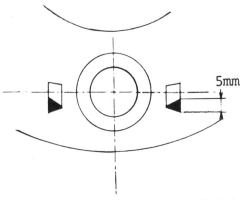

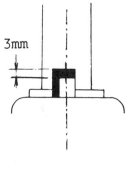

Modified YJ1 fork stops

Ignition Timing	2.0 mm BTDC
Spark Plug	B8E or B9E*
Carburetor-	
Main Jet	#110
Jet Needle	4J4 – 3 stage
Slide Cutaway	2.0
Fuel/Oil Ratio	15:1

*B8HC or B9HC if stock cylinder head is used.

YG1 (For Off-Road Racing)

CYLINDER HEAD

Use the GYT cylinder head or perform the following modifications on the stock head:

1. Machine 3.5 mm off the bottom of the head.

2. Remove approximately 2.0 mm from the bottom edge of the cooling fins.

3. Taper the bottom edge of the combustion chamber approximately 20°.

CYLINDER

Use the chrome-plated GYT cylinder or perform the following modifications on the stock cylinder:

1. Remove 2.0 mm from the top of the transfer ports.

2. Remove 3.5 mm from the top of the exhaust port.

3. Enlarge the exhaust port passage as shown in the illustration.

4. Bevel the reshaped ports to eliminate any rough edges.

PISTON AND RINGS

Use the GYT piston or modify the stock piston by cutting a 5.0 mm × 26.0 mm notch in the piston skirt directly opposite the exhaust port (facing the transfer port).

Use standard rings in a modified stock cylinder and cast-iron rings in the GYT cylinder.

NOTE: Ring groove width is 1.5 mm.

PISTON FIT

The piston-to-cylinder wall clearance should be 0.04–0.05 mm in the GYT cylinder and 0.05–0.06 mm in the stock cast-iron cylinder.

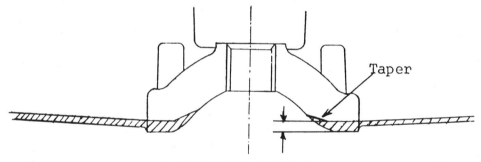

Modified YG1 cylinder head

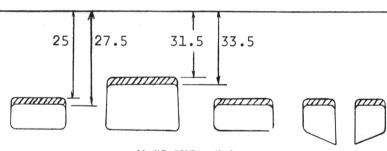

Modified YG1 cylinder

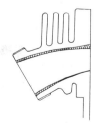

Modified YG1 exhaust port

CARBURETOR

Replace the stock VM15SC carburetor with a Mikuni VM22SC (standard on the YA6).

ROTARY-VALVE

Use the GYT valve or modify the stock valve by increasing the intake duration to 147° and widening the cutaway as shown in the illustration.

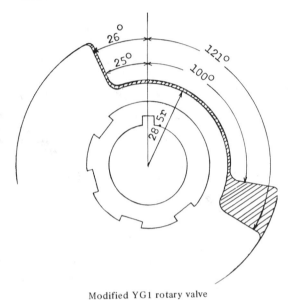

Modified YG1 rotary valve

ROTARY-VALVE COVER

Use the GYT valve cover and an O-ring from a standard YA6 cover. The stock cover cannot be modified to accommodate the larger carburetor.

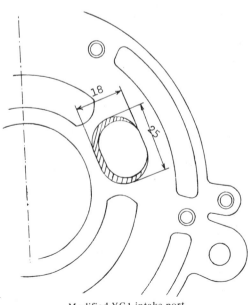

Modified YG1 intake port

CRANKCASE INTAKE PORT

Enlarge the intake port as shown in the illustration and taper the bottom edge 7°. Mount the GYT or modified rotary valve, valve cover, and carburetor on the crankcase. Then check the alignment of the entire intake passage. There should be no steps or rough areas at the joining seams.

CRANKCASE COVER

Only the GYT crankcase cover can be used. The stock cover cannot be modified to fit the larger carburetor.

CARBURETOR COVER

The GYT cover must be used in conjunction with the GYT valve and crankcase covers.

CARBURETOR CAP

The GYT carburetor cap and cap plate must be used.

EXHAUST SYSTEM

Use a GYT expansion chamber or one made to the same dimensions. The stock muffler cannot be used.

ELECTRICAL SYSTEM

Remove the magneto lighting coil and all unnecessary accessories, lights, and wiring.

SUSPENSION

Use the stock front fork with GYT or YG1T springs. Increase the fork's damping effect by filling the fork legs with 30 to 50W oil.

Use GYT or YG1T rear shock absorbers. If necessary, modify the shock mounting points to accommodate a larger rear wheel sprocket (see YJ1 illustration).

TUNING SPECIFICATIONS

Use these settings as a starting point, then tailor them to suit varying conditions.

Ignition Timing	2.3 mm BTDC
Spark Plug	B8E or B9E*
Carburetor	
Main Jet	#260
Jet Needle	#22 M3−3 stage
Slide Cutaway	2.5
Fuel/Oil Ratio	15:1

*B8HC or B9HC with modified stock cylinder head.

YL2/C (For Off-Road Racing)

CYLINDER HEAD

Use the stock cylinder head.

CYLINDER

Use the stock cylinder.

PISTON AND RINGS

Use the stock piston and rings.

PISTON FIT

Piston-to-cylinder wall clearance should be 0.05–0.06 mm.

CARBURETOR

Replace the standard VM17SC with a Mikuni VM22SC (stock on the YA6).

ROTARY-VALVE

Use the stock rotary valve.

CRANKCASE INTAKE PORT

The crankcase intake port need not be modified.

ROTARY-VALVE COVER

Only the GYT rotary valve cover can be used.

CRANKCASE AND CARBURETOR COVERS

Only the GYT covers can be used. The stock covers cannot be modified to accommodate the larger carburetor.

CARBURETOR CAP

Use only the GYT carburetor cap.

EXHAUST SYSTEM

Use the GYT expansion chamber assembly. The stock muffler cannot be modified.

ELECTRICAL SYSTEM

Use the GYT magneto and the stock ignition coil. Remove any unnecessary accessories, lights, and wiring.

SUSPENSION

Use the stock forks with heavy oil (30 to 50W) and the rear shock absorbers set at the highest spring tension.

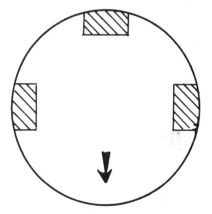

YL2 notched piston

*YL2 HIGH RPM POWER
(FOR ROADRACING)*

The previous modifications increase power mostly in the lower- and mid-rpm ranges. If more power is needed at higher rpm, perform the following modifications:

1. Remove 7.0 mm all the way around the piston skirt.
2. Cut three notches in the piston crown as shown in the illustration.

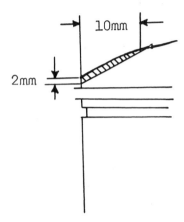

YL2 piston notch dimensions

3. Remove 2.0 mm from the top of the exhaust port.
4. Cut 9.0 mm off the carburetor air horn.

Tuning Specifications

Ignition Timing	2.0 mm BTDC
Spark Plug	B9HN
Carburetor	
Main Jet	#170*
Jet Needle	4J6–2 stage
Slide Cutaway	2.5

*160 w/cylinder modification

YL1 (For Roadracing)

CYLINDER HEADS

Use the GYT cylinder heads or modify the stock heads by performing the following:

1. Remove 1.5 mm from the bottom of the heads.
2. Taper the bottom of the combustion chambers 20°.

CYLINDERS

Use the GYT cylinders or modify the stock cylinders to the specifications shown in the illustration.

PISTON AND RINGS

Use the GYT pistons and ring set if the GYT cylinders are used. If the stock cylinders are

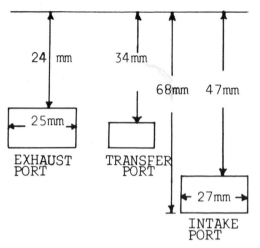

Modified YL1 cylinder

used, remove 5.0 mm from the piston skirt and use the standard top ring only.

OIL PUMP

Remove the oil pump and install the GYT cover plate. Plug the delivery line fittings at the base of the cylinders (if stock cylinders are used).

CARBURETORS

Replace the stock VM16SC carburetors with VM18 Mikunis.

CLUTCH

Install the GYT clutch parts or use the entire YA6 clutch assembly.

LARGE END CONNECTING ROD BEARING

If GYT components are being used throughout, install the GYT bearing. It is considerably stronger than the stock bearing and will increase the engine's high rpm capabilities.

EXHAUST SYSTEM

Install the GYT expansion chambers if GYT parts are being used throughout. If modified stock parts (connecting rod bearing, cylinder, etc.) are being used, have expansion chambers made to the specifications shown in the illustration.

ELECTRICAL SYSTEM

Install the GYT magneto assembly or perform the following on the stock unit and run a "total loss" ignition system:

1. Remove the field windings from the generator case.
2. Turn the generator armature on a lathe and machine it down to the bare shaft.
3. Disconnect the armature and field wires.
NOTE: This total loss ignition system uses only the battery, points, and ignition coil. There is no charging circuit.

SUSPENSION

Use the stock front fork with YG1T springs and increase the damping by filling the fork legs with 30 to 50W oil. Use the stock rear shock absorbers set at the highest spring tension position.

TUNING SPECIFICATIONS

Use the following as a starting point, then modify the settings as necessary.

Ignition Timing	2.0 mm BTDC
Spark Plug	B10E*
Carburetor	
Main Jet	NA
Needle Jet	NA
Slide Cutaway	NA
Fuel/Oil Ratio	15:1

*B10H, if the modified stock cylinder head is used.

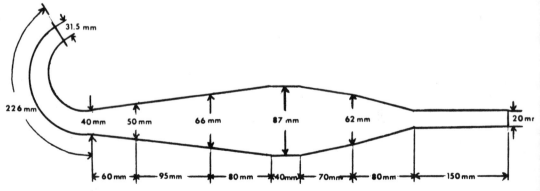

YL1 expansion chamber dimensions

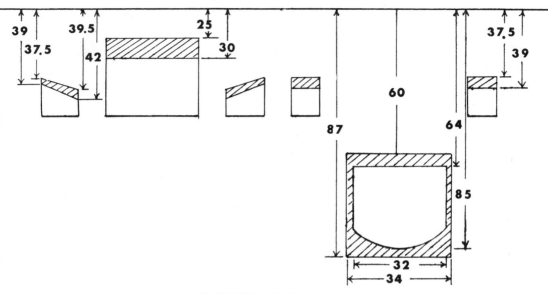

Modified DS6 cylinder

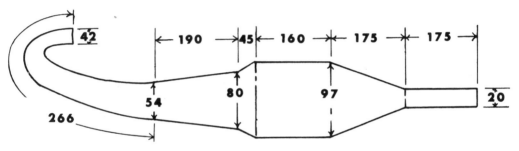

DS6 expansion chamber dimensions

DS6 (For Roadracing)

CYLINDER HEAD

Machine the bottom of the head until the combustion chamber capacity is 11.3 cc. Taper the bottom edge to the original configuration.

CYLINDERS

Remove the shaded areas in the illustration. This porting arrangement is the same as that on the factory TD2 roadracer.

PISTONS

Use TD2 pistons which are 54 mm in length. Standard piston length is 63 mm.

OIL PUMP

Remove the oil pump and run a 15:1 fuel/oil mixture.

CARBURETORS

Install the 30 mm TD2 carburetors.

EXHAUST SYSTEM

Use the TD2 expansion chambers or have a pair made to the dimensions given in the illustration.

TUNING SPECIFICATIONS

See the TD2 specifications.

Factory Roadracing Models

Model	TD1A	TD1B	TD1C	TD2A	TD2B	TR2A	TR2B
Horsepower @ RPM	35 @ 10,000	35 @ 10,000	38 @ 10,000	44@ 10,000	44@ 10,000	54 @ 9,500	54 @ 9,500
Torque @ RPM	19.53 @ 9,000	19.53 @ 9,000	20 @ 9,500	22.9 @ 9,500	22.9 @ 9,500	30.2 @ 9,000	30.2 @ 9,000
Bore & Stroke (mm)	56 x 50 (2)	56 x 50 (2)	56 x 50 (2)	56 x 50 (2)	56 x 50 (2)	61 x 59.6	61 x 59.6
Capacity	246cc 15 cu in.	246cc 15 cu in.	246cc 15 cu in.	246cc 15 cu in.	246cc 15 cu in.	347cc	347cc
Net Weight (Approx.)	275.6 lbs	275.6 lbs	310 lbs	231 lbs	231 lbs	253 lbs	253 lbs
Compression Ratio	9:1	8.1:1	8.1:1	7.6:1	7.6:1	6.5:1	6.5:1
Ignit. Timing BTDC (mm) Ret.	—	—	—	—	—	—	—
Adv.	2.1mm ± 0.03	2.0mm ± 0.03	2.0mm ± 0.03	2.0mm	2.0mm	2.0mm	2.0mm
Cont. Break. Pt. Gap Set. (mm) (in)	.25–.30mm 0.10–.011 in.	.25–.30mm 0.10–.011 in.	.25–.30mm .010–.011 in.	.3–.35mm .011–.013 in.	.3–.35mm .011–.013 in.	.3–.4mm .012–.015 in.	.3–.4mm .012–.015 in.
Spark Plug & Gap (mm)	B-IOEN .6–.7mm	B-IOEN .6–.7mm	B-IOEN .6–.7mm	B-IOEN	B-IOEN	B-IOEN	B-IOEN
Volt. Reg. Adj. (Volt/rpm-no load)							
Cutout Relay Adj. (Cut in volt.)	Magneto	Magneto	Magneto	Magneto	Magneto	Magneto	Magneto
Condenser Cap. (Microfarad)	0.22μf	0.22μf	0.22μf	0.22μf	0.22μf	0.22μf	0.22μf
Piston Skirt Clear. (mm) (in)	.060–.065mm .0024–.0026 in.	.045–.050mm .0018–.0020 in.	.045–.050mm .0018–.0020 in.	.040–.045mm .0016–.0018 in.	.040–.045mm .0016–.0018 in.	.040–.045mm .0016–.0018 in.	.040–.045mm .0016–.0018 in.
Carburetor Type & Mfr.	VM276 Mikuni (2)	VM276 Mikuni (2)	VM276 Mikuni (2)	VM30SC Mikuni (2)	VM30SC Mikuni (2)	VM34SC Mikuni (2)	VM34SC Mikuni (2)
Main Jet (M.J.)	#200	#190	#190	#280	#280	#380	#380
Air Jet (A.J.)	2.0	—	2.0	2.0	2.0	2.0	2.0
Needle Jet (N.J.)	Q-3	Q-3	Q-3	O-6	O-6	O-6	O-6
Jet Needle –clip pos. (J.N.)	6A1-3	6A1-3	8F3-2	6F4-4	6F4-2	6F5-4	6F5-4
Cutaway (C.A.)	3.5	3.5	3.5	3.0	3.0	1.5	1.5

	#25	#25	#25	#50	#50	#60	#60
Pilot Jet (P.J.)	#25	#25	#25	#50	#50	#60	#60
Air Screw (Turns out) (A.S.)	1½	1½	1½	1½	1½	1½	1½
Starter Jet (S.J.)	—	—	—	—	—	—	—
Float Level (mm) (F.L.)	25.5mm	25.5mm	25.5mm	25.5mm	25.5mm	25.5mm	25.5mm
Air Filter Type	None	None	None	None	None	None	None
Prim. Reduct. Ratio & Method	65/20 3.250 gear	65/20 3.250 gear	65/20 3.250 gear	N.A. 3.70 gear	N.A. 3.70 gear	N.A. 2.704 gear	N.A. 2.704 gear
Sec. Reduct. Ratio & Method	34/17 2.000 chain	34/17 2.000 chain	34/17 2.000 chain	20/30 ≈ 34 chain	20/30 ≈ 34 chain	16/33 ≈ 35 chain	16/33 ≈ 35 chain
Trans. Gear Ratios 1st (intern.) (No. teeth) (Overall)	2.500 35/14 16.250	2.267 N.A. 14.736	2.267 N.A. 14.736	2.000 26/13 7.40	2.000 26/13 7.40	1.714 24/14 4.64	1.714 24/14 4.64
2nd	1.579 N.A. 10.264	1.579 N.A. 10.264	1.579 N.A. 10.264	1.533 23/15 5.67	1.533 23/15 5.67	1.293 22/17 3.50	1.293 22/17 3.50
3rd	1.227 27/22 7.976	1.227 27/22 7.976	1.227 27/22 7.976	1.236 21/17 4.57	1.236 21/17 4.57	1.053 20/19 2.85	1.053 20/19 2.85
4th	1.042 25/24 6.773	1.042 25/24 6.773	1.042 25/24 6.773	1.053 20/19 3.90	1.053 20/19 3.90	0.900 18/20 2.44	0.900 18/20 2.44
5th	0.924 24/26 6.006	0.924 24/26 6.006	0.924 24/26 6.006	0.951 19/20 3.52	0.951 19/20 3.52	0.818 18/22 2.21	0.818 18/22 2.21
Trans. Oil Capacity (qt)	1.5	1.5	1.5	1.7	1.7	1.4	1.4
Oil Tank or Eng. Sump Cap. (qt)	5.54	—	—	1.9	1.9	1.9	1.9
Fuel Tank Cap. (gal)	—	5.54	5.54	6.1	6.1	6.1	6.1
Fr. Fork Oil Cap. (each leg)	195cc 6.6 oz	195cc 6.6 oz	195cc 6.6 oz	215cc 7.3 oz	215cc 7.3 oz	215cc 7.3 oz	215cc 7.3 oz
Tire Size (Front)	2.50 x 18	2.75 x 18	2.75 x 18	2.75 x 18	2.75 x 18	3.00 x 18	3.00 x 18
(Rear)	2.75 x 18	3.00 x 18	3.00 x 18	3.00 x 18	3.00 x 18	3.00 x 18	3.00 x 18
Tire Pressure (lbs) (Front)	—	—	—	—	—	—	—
(Rear)	—	—	—	—	—	—	—
Drive Chain Tens. (Up & down freeplay)	—	—	—	—	—	—	—
Oil Pump Stroke Adj. Min. (mm)	—	—	—	No Adjustment	No Adjustment	No Adjustment	No Adjustment
Max. (mm)	—	—	—	No Adjustment	No Adjustment	No Adjustment	No Adjustment
Auto. Cable Adj. (Throt. pos.)	—	—	—	No Adjustment	No Adjustment	No Adjustment	No Adjustment

Factory Motocross Models

Model	AT1B-MX	AT1C-MX	YDS2M	YDS3M	DT1C-MX	DT1E-MX	RT1-MX	RT1B-MX
Horsepower @ RPM	18.2 @ 8500	18.0 @ 8,500	N.A.	N.A.	30 @ 7000	30 @ 7,000	30 @ 6,000	36 @ 6,500
Torque @ RPM	14.8 @ 7500	11.4 @ 7,500	N.A.	N.A.	22.4 @ 6500	22.4 @ 6,500	26.0 @ 5,500	28.7 @ 6,500
Bore & Stroke (mm)	56 × 50	56 × 50	56 × 50 (2)	56 × 50 (2)	70 × 64	70 × 64	80 × 70	80 × 70
Engine Displacement	123cc 7.50 cu in.	123cc 7.51 cu in.	246cc 15 cu in.	246cc 15 cu in.	246cc 15 cu in.	246cc 15.0 cu in.	352cc 21.50 cu in.	351cc 21.4 cu in.
Net Weight (Appx.)	202 lbs	202 lbs	N.A.	N.A.	229 lbs	232 lbs	242 lbs	242 lbs
Compression Ratio	8.0:1	8.0:1	9.0:1	8.8:1	8.2:1	8.2:1	7.5:1	7.2:1
Ignit. Timing BTDC (mm) Ret.	—	—	—	—	—	—	—	—
Adv.	2.0mm ± .1	2.0mm ± .1	1.7mm	2.0mm	2.3mm	2.3mm ± .1	3.4mm ± .1	2.9mm ± .1
Cont. Break. Pt. Gap Set. (mm)	.3-.35mm	.30-.40mm	.25-.30mm	.25-.30mm	.3-.35mm	.30-.40mm	.3-.35mm	.30-.40mm
Cont. Break. Pt. Gap Set. (in.)	0.011-0.13 in.	.012-.015 in.	.010-.011 in.	.010-.011 in.	.011-.013 in.	.012-.015 in.	.011-.013 in.	.012-.015 in.
Spark Plug & Gap (mm)	B-9E .5-.6mm	B-9EN .5-.6mm	B-10EN .6-.7mm	B-8EN, B-9EN .5-.6mm	B-10EN .5-.6mm	B-10EN .5-.6mm	B-9EN .5-.6mm	B-9EN .5-.6mm
Volt. Reg. Adj. (Volts @ rpm—no ld.)	Magneto	Magneto	Magneto	Magneto	Magneto	Magneto	Magneto	Magneto
Cutout Relay Adj. (Cut in volt.)	0.3µf ± 10%							
Condenser Cap. (Microfarad)	0.22µf	0.22µf	0.22µf	0.22µf	0.22µf	0.22µf	0.22µf	0.22µf
Piston Skirt Clear. (mm)	.04-.05mm	.040-.050mm	.060-.0605mm	.055-.060mm	.040-.050mm	.045-.050mm	.055-.060mm	.055-.060mm
Piston Skirt Clear. (inch)	.0016-.002 in.	.0016-.0020 in.	.0024-.0026 in.	.0022-.0024 in.	.0016-.0020 in.	.0018-.0020 in.	.0022-.0024 in.	.0022-.0024 in.
Carburetor Type & Mfr.	VM26SH Mikuni	VM26SH Mikuni	VM24H Mik. (2)	VM24SC Mik. (2)	VM30SH	VM30SH Mikuni	VM34SH	VM34SH Mikuni
Main Jet (M.J.)	#190	#190	#110	#120	#220	#180	#320	#310
Air Jet (A.J.)	0.5	0.5	0.5	0.5	0.5	0.5	0.5	0.5
Needle Jet (N.J.)	N-8	O-2	O-0	O-0	O-4	O-2	P-5	P-0
Jet Needle—clip pos. (J.N.)	4F15-3	4F15-2	24A1-4	24J1-3	5D5-4	5DP7-3	ED-4	WE-2
Cutaway (C.A.)	1.5	1.5	2.5	2.0	3.5	3.5	2.0	2.5

	#30	#30	#40	#20	#80	#80	#30	#60
Pilot Jet (P.J.)	#30	#30	#40	#20	#80	#80	#30	#60
Air Screw (Turns out) (A.S.)	1½	1½	1½	1½	½	1.0	1¼	1½
Starter Jet (S.J.)	#40	#40	#60	#60	#60	#60	#60	#60
Float Level (mm) (F.L.)	25.5mm	25.5mm	25.5mm	25.5mm	25.5mm	25.5mm	25.5mm	8.5mm
Air Filter Type	Wet foam rub.	Wet foam rub.	Paper	Paper	Wet foam rub.	Wet foam rub.	Wet foam rub.	Wet foam rub.
Pri. Reduct. Ratio & Method	74/19 3.895 gear	74/19 3.895 gear	65/20 3.250 gear	65/20 3.250 gear	65/21 3.095 gear	65/21 3.095 gear	65/21 3.095 gear	65/21 3.095 gear
Sec. Reduct. Ratio & Method	45/15 3.000 chain	45/15 3.000 chain	45/15 3.000 chain	41/16 2.563 chain	44/14 3.143 chain	44/14 3.143 chain	39/15 2.600 chain	44/15 2.933 chain
Trans. Gear Ratios								
1st (Intern.) (No. teeth) (Overall)	2.833 34/12 33.10	2.833 34/12 33.10	2.500 35/14 24.374	2.500 35/14 20.825	2.250 36/16 21.888	2.250 36/16 21.89	2.250 36/16 18.106	2.250 36/16 18.11
2nd (Intern.) (No. teeth) (Overall)	1.875 30/16 21.91	1.875 30/16 21.90	1.667 30/18 16.249	1.667 30/18 13.886	1.650 33/20 16.051	1.650 33/20 16.05	1.650 33/20 13.278	1.650 33/20 13.28
3rd (Intern.) (No. teeth) (Overall)	1.368 26/19 15.99	1.368 26/19 15.98	1.227 27/22 11.966	1.227 27/22 10.221	1.261 29/23 12.267	1.261 29/23 12.27	1.261 29/23 10.147	1.261 29/23 10.15
4th (Intern.) (No. teeth) (Overall)	1.091 24/22 12.76	1.091 24/22 12.76	0.960 24/25 9.359	1.042 25/24 8.680	1.000 26/26 9.728	1.000 26/26 9.73	1.000 26/26 8.047	1.000 26/26 8.05
5th (Intern.) (No. teeth) (Overall)	0.957 22/23 11.18	0.957 22/23 11.18	0.750 21/28 7.300	0.924 24/26 7.697	.793 23/29 7.714	.793 23/29 7.71	.793 23/29 6.381	.793 23/29 6.38
Trans. Oil Capacity (qt)	.78	.80	1.5	1.5	1.06	1.06	1.06	1.06
Oil Tank or Eng. Sump Cap. (qt)	1.3	1.3	—	—	1.7	1.7	1.7	1.7
Fuel Tank Cap. (U.S. gal)	1.9	1.9	4.13	4.13	2.5	2.5	2.5	2.5
Fr. Fork Oil Cap. (Each leg)	145–160cc 4.9–5.5 oz	145–160cc 4.9–5.4 oz	200cc 6.7 oz	200cc 6.7 oz	210cc 7.1 oz	210cc 7.1 oz	210cc 7.1 oz	175cc 5.9 oz
Tire Size (Front)	3.00 × 18	3.25 × 18	3.00 × 18	3.00 × 18	2.75 × 21 knobby	2.75 × 21 knobby	2.75 × 21 knobby	2.75 × 21 knobby
(Rear)	3.50 × 18	3.50 × 18	3.25 × 18	3.25 × 18	4.00 × 18 knobby	4.00 × 18 knobby	4.00 × 18 knobby	4.00 × 18 knobby
Tire Pressure (lbs) (Front)	14	14	—	—	14	13	14	13
(Rear)	17	17	—	—	17	16	17	16
Drive Chain Tens. (Up & down freeplay)	20mm 25/32 in.	20mm 25/32 in.	20mm 25/32 in.	20mm 25/32 in.	20mm 25/32 in.	20mm 25/32 in.	20mm 25/32 in.	20mm 25/32 in.
Oil Pump Stroke Adj. Min. (mm)	.20-.25mm	.20-.25mm	—	—	.20-.25mm	.20-.25mm	.20-.25mm	.20-.25mm
Max. (mm)	2.05	1.85-2.05mm	—	—	1.85-2.05mm	1.85-2.05mm	1.85-2.05mm	1.85-2.05mm
Autolube Cable Adj. (Throt. pos.)	At idle	At idle	—	—	At idle	At idle	At idle	At idle

10 ● Troubleshooting

Two-Stroke Performance Troubleshooting

DIFFICULT OR NO STARTING

Possible Causes	Inspection and/or Remedy
1. IGNITION SYSTEM	
a. Weak or dead battery.	Check for a bright blue spark by shorting the spark plug against the cylinder cooling fins and kicking the engine over. If there is no spark, or it is very weak, check battery output, then clean and tighten terminal connections.
b. Bridged, fouled or dirty spark plug.	Clean or replace. Make sure the plug is of the correct heat range.
c. Incorrect spark plug gap.	Reset.
d. Burned, dirty or incorrectly gapped ignition points.	Clean or replace. Set correct gap.
e. Incorrect ignition timing.	Reset.
f. Faulty condenser.	Test condenser capacity (see Electrical Specifications) and replace if necessary.
g. Faulty magneto, generator or alternator.	Test voltage output and isolate trouble source as described in Electrical Systems.
h. Faulty wiring harness.	Check for short circuits, poor grounds, etc., and repair as necessary.
2. FUEL SYSTEM	
a. No fuel delivery.	Check fuel level and switch to reserve. Disconnect the delivery line at the carburetor and make sure there is free fuel flow. If not, look for a clogged gas tank vent, fuel petcock or delivery line.
b. Stuck carburetor float.	Disassemble the float bowl and make sure that the float operates freely and that the float needle seat is free from obstruction.
c. Poor quality fuel.	Inspect the spark plugs and if yellow brown sulphur deposits are evident, flush and refill the fuel tank with fresh good quality fuel.
3. LOSS OF COMPRESSION	Check cylinder compression as described in Tune-Up Analysis.
a. Loose spark plug.	Usually caused by over-torqueing the plug and stripping the cylinder head threads. Either a HeliCoil insert or a new cylinder head will be required.

Two-Stroke Performance Troubleshooting—continued

Difficult or No Starting—Continued

Possible Causes	Inspection and/or Remedy
b. Loose cylinder head.	Make sure the head is correctly fitted and torqued.
c. Broken head gasket.	Replace.
d. Worn piston rings.	Replace.
e. Excessive piston to cylinder wall clearance.	Replace the piston and rings; rebore or replace the cylinder. (See Engine and Transmission.)
f. Leaking crankcase seal.	Replace. (See Engine and Transmission.)
g. Warped or sheared rotary valve disc.	Replace. (See Engine and Transmission.)
4. FUEL MIXTURE (Hard Starting)	See Tune-Up Analysis and determine if the carburetion is lean or rich. Make sure adjustments are correct and the air cleaner isn't dirty.
a. Lean mixture.	Check the intake manifold and inspect the throttle stop screw(s), starter jet(s), air screw(s) and pilot jet.
b. Rich mixture.	Inspect the air screw, air jet, needle jet and air cleaner element.

HARD STARTING OR IRREGULAR IDLE

Possible Causes	Inspection and/or Remedy
1. IGNITION SYSTEM	
a. Weak battery output.	Check battery voltage and make sure all connections are tight and clean.
b. Dirty or incorrect spark plug.	Check plug condition, heat range and electrode gap.
c. Incorrect ignition timing.	Reset.
d. Dirty or worn-out points.	Replace the points and check for any signs of oil leakage around the breaker cam. Wet points usually indicate a faulty oil seal.
e. Faulty condenser.	If the points were badly burned or discolored, its very likely that a bad condenser is the cause. Replace it and be safe.
f. Faulty automatic advance.	If the engine backfires when starting, inspect the advance mechanism and make sure it is functioning properly
g. Faulty magneto.	Check the slip ring and pickup for grease, dirt, etc., and clean as necessary.
2. FUEL SYSTEM	
a. Incorrectly adjusted carburetor idle circuit.	Check all parts associated with the idle circuit (see Fuel Systems). Clean and readjust as necessary.
b. Clogged carburetor fuel jets.	If the bike has been stored or left sitting for some time, there is the possibility of sediment or oil residue obstructing fuel flow through the main and needle jets. Clean all the jets in solvent and blow them dry with compressed air.
3. DIRTY AIR CLEANER	Clean or replace.
4. EXCESSIVE CARBON BUILD-UP	Decarbonize the engine as described in Maintenance.

MISFIRE DURING ACCELERATION FROM IDLE

Possible Causes	Inspection and/or Remedy
1. INCORRECT IDLE MIXTURE	A misfire while accelerating from a standstill is often caused by too rich an idle mixture. Readjust the idle mixture and, if necessary, remove and clean the jets.
2. WATER IN CARBURETOR FLOAT BOWL OR FUEL PETCOCK.	Drain and flush with fresh gasoline.
3. FAULTY SPARK PLUG.	Look for signs of bridging, tracking or flashover (see Tune-Up Analysis). Sandblast or replace the plug.

Two-Stroke Performance Troubleshooting—continued

MISFIRE AT A GIVEN THROTTLE OPENING ONLY

Possible Causes	Inspection and/or Remedy
1. FAULTY CARBURETOR	Disassemble and inspect all carburetor parts for nicks, scratches, etc. Pay particular attention to the needle jet and jet needle.

MISFIRE AT A GIVEN RPM ONLY

Possible Causes	Inspection and/or Remedy
1. FAULTY AUTOMATIC ADVANCE	This type of misfire is usually caused by the automatic advance unit getting hung up. Inspect the mechanism and make sure it operates properly and smoothly.

INTERMITTENT MISFIRE

Possible Causes	Inspection and/or Remedy
1. IGNITION SYSTEM	Check all items in the ignition/electrical system: points, plugs, high tension wires, grounds and wiring harness connections.

MISFIRE UNDER LOAD

Possible Causes	Inspection and/or Remedy
1. FAULTY SPARK PLUG	Inspect the plug for signs of overheating. Install cooler plug, if necessary.
2. INCORRECT IGNITION TIMING	Make sure timing is correct because it becomes more critical as load increases.
3. DIRTY AIR CLEANER	Clean or replace.
4. INCORRECT FUEL MIXTURE	Make sure that the fuel mixture is not too rich. Check main jet size.
5. POOR QUALITY FUEL	Check plug condition and, if necessary, drain and replace the fuel.

HIGH SPEED MISFIRE

Possible Causes	Inspection and/or Remedy
1. IGNITION SYSTEM	
a. Faulty spark plug.	Check plug condition and heat range.
b. Incorrect spark plug gap.	Reset.
c. Faulty condenser.	Test and, if necessary, replace.
d. Faulty ignition coil.	Test and, if necessary, replace.
e. Faulty high tension leads	Inspect the leads for signs of corona discharge: soft rubber.
2. FUEL SYSTEM	
a. Incorrect fuel mixture.	Inspect the main and needle jet for any nicks, etc. Also make sure the jet needle clip is properly positioned and the needle is not damaged.
b. Incorrect float level.	Reset.
c. Air leak.	Inspect the fuel induction passage and make sure there is no place for air to enter other than the carburetor throat.
3. LOSS OF COMPRESSION	Measure cylinder compression as described in Tune-Up Analysis.
a. Broken head gasket.	Replace.
b. Broken cylinder base gasket	Replace.
c. Leaking crankcase oil seal.	Replace.

Two-Stroke Performance Troubleshooting—continued

High Speed Misfire—Continued

Possible Causes	Inspection and/or Remedy
4. DIRTY AIR CLEANER	Clean or replace.
5. CARBON BUILD-UP IN HEAD AND/OR EXHAUST PASSAGE	Decarbonize.

Autolube Troubleshooting

POOR OR NO OIL DELIVERY

Possible Causes	Inspection and/or Remedy
1. AIR BUBBLES IN OIL LINE OR PUMP	Bleed the pump and check for any signs of leakage.

PUMP OPERATES CONSTANTLY AT MINIMUM STROKE

Possible Causes	Inspection and/or Remedy
1. BROKEN PUMP CABLE	Replace or repair.
2. BROKEN PULLEY GUIDE PIN	Replace guide pin or pump.

NO PLUNGER ACTION

Possible Causes	Inspection and/or Remedy
1. BROKEN PLUNGER GUIDE PIN	Replace guide pin or pump.
2. OBSTRUCTED GUIDE PIN GROOVE	Clean.

Four-Stroke Performance Troubleshooting

DIFFICULT OR NO STARTING

Possible Causes	Inspection and/or Remedy
1. IGNITION SYSTEM	
a. Faulty spark plug.	Clean or replace.
b. Incorrect spark plug gap.	Reset.
c. Faulty ignition points.	Clean or replace.
d. Incorrect point gap.	Reset.
e. Incorrect ignition timing.	Reset.
f. Faulty condenser.	A faulty condenser will usually be indicated by badly burned or discolored points. Test condenser capacity and insulation as described in Electrical Systems, then replace if necessary.
g. Faulty ignition coil.	Inspect and test the ignition coil as described in Electrical Systems.
h. Broken brown or red ignition wires.	Test horn and stoplight. No operation indicates a possible broken wire.
i. Faulty main switch.	Check the switch for shorts or broken wires.
j. Blown fuse.	Replace.
k. Weak or no battery output.	Test battery specific gravity, then recharge or replace.
2. FUEL SYSTEM	Disconnect the delivery line at the carburetor and check for free fuel flow. If there is none, check the tank cap vent, petcock and fuel line; if the flow is normal, check carburetor fuel level and equalizer tube.
3. LOSS OF COMPRESSION	Check compression on each cylinder as described in Tune-Up Analysis.
a. Incorrectly adjusted valve tappet.	Reset.
b. Incorrect valve timing.	Adjust the cam chain and make sure the camshaft is properly installed.
c. Broken cylinder head gasket.	Replace.
d. Faulty valve seats.	Repair. See Engine and Transmission.
e. Worn piston rings.	This condition is usually indicated by blue exhaust smoke being developed over a period of time.
f. Worn cylinder.	Rebore. See Engine and Transmission.
g. Worn valve guides.	Replace. See Engine and Transmission.
h. Leaking guide seals.	Replace.

POOR IDLE AND/OR LOW SPEED PERFORMANCE

Possible Causes	Inspection and/or Remedy
1. IGNITION SYSTEM	
a. Faulty spark plug.	Clean or replace.
b. Incorrect spark plug gap	Reset.
c. Faulty ignition points.	Clean or replace. Reset gap.
d. Incorrect ignition timing.	Reset.
e. Weak spark.	Test ignition coil and condenser as described in Electrical Systems.
f. Weak or dead battery.	Check horn and stoplight for broken wire. Recharge battery if hydrometer reading is low.
2. FUEL SYSTEM	
a. Clogged fuel tank vent.	Clean.

Four-Stroke Performance Troubleshooting—continued

Poor Idle and/or Low Speed Performance

Possible Causes	Inspection and/or Remedy
b. Clogged fuel petcock.	Clean.
c. Carburetor low speed or idle system inoperative.	Clean and repair as necessary.
d. Clogged or incorrectly adjusted pilot screw.	Clean or readjust.
e. Incorrect carburetor float level.	Adjust.
f. Faulty starter jet.	Make sure the jet is opening and closing correctly.

POOR MID-RANGE AND/OR HIGH SPEED PERFORMANCE

Possible Causes	Inspection and/or Remedy
1. IGNITION SYSTEM	
a. Faulty spark plug.	Check plug condition and heat range.
b. Faulty automatic advance.	Check advance mechanism counterweights and make sure they pivot properly and smoothly.
c. Incorrect ignition timing.	Reset.
d. Incorrect point gap.	Reset.
2. FUEL SYSTEM	
a. Faulty carburetor butterfly valve.	Adjust or repair.
b. Dirty air cleaner.	Clean or replace.
c. Incorrect float level.	Readjust.
d. Leaking carburetor vacuum diaphragm.	Observe the diaphragm piston during operation, then replace if necessary.
e. Incorrect carburetor alignment.	Make sure the carburetors are in line and parallel to the cylinder cooling fins.
f. Incorrect fuel mixture.	Check main jet size and jet needle clip position. Set up carburetors to standard specifications, then determine if any jetting changes are needed by making spark plug readings (see Tune-Up Analysis).
g. Faulty starter jets.	Make sure the jets are fully closed when starter lever is in the "off" position.
3. LOSS OF COMPRESSION	Check compression on each cylinder as described in Tune-Up Analysis.
a. Weak or broken valve spring.	Test valve spring pressure and replace if necessary.
b. Incorrect valve timing.	Tighten the cam chain and make sure the camshaft is correctly installed.
c. Worn or broken piston rings.	Replace.

OVERHEATING

Possible Causes	Inspection and/or Remedy
1. IGNITION SYSTEM	
a. Incorrect ignition timing.	Reset timing and make sure the automatic advance mechanism is functioning properly.
b. Incorrect spark plug.	Make plug readings and, if necessary, install one-step colder plugs.
2. FUEL SYSTEM	
a. Incorrect fuel mixture.	Check for any air leaks in the induction tract that could cause a lean fuel mixture.

Four-Stroke Performance Troubleshooting—continued

Overheating—Continued

Possible Causes	Inspection and/or Remedy
b. Poor quality fuel.	This condition is usually indicated by detonation, or "pinging," and sulphur deposits on the spark plug.
3. LUBRICATION SYSTEM a. Insufficient amount of oil.	Check and refill.
b. Improper weight oil.	Overheating is often caused by oil that becomes too thin when the engine is operating at normal or slightly above normal temperatures. Drain and replace.
c. Faulty oil pump.	This is an unusual situation because the oil pump seldom fails. If this is the case, however, the tachometer would also be inoperative.
d. Clogged oil passages.	If this appears to be the problem, the engine will have to be disassembled and all the oil passages flushed and blown out with compressed air.

EXCESSIVE EXHAUST SMOKE

Possible Causes	Inspection and/or Remedy
1. TOO MUCH ENGINE OIL	Check and drain.
2. PLUGGED OIL BREATHER	Check and clean.
3. WORN CYLINDER AND/OR PISTON RINGS	Rebore and replace.
4. WORN VALVE GUIDES	Replace.
5. CRACKED VALVE GUIDE SEALS	Replace.